I'd Hate Myself in the Morning

RING LARDNER, JR.

I'd Hate Myself in the Morning

a memoir

THUNDER'S MOUTH PRESS / NATION BOOKS
NEW YORK

Published by
Thunder's Mouth Press/Nation Books
841 Broadway, Fourth Floor
New York, NY 10003

Nation Books is a co-publishing venture of the Nation Institute
and Avalon Publishing Group Incorporated.

Library of Congress Cataloging-in-Publication Data

Lardner, Ring, 1915-
I'd hate myself in the morning / by Ring Lardner, Jr.
      p. cm.
ISBN 1-56025-296-0
1. Lardner, Ring, 1915- 2. Author, American—20th century—Biography.
3. Screenwriters—United States—Biography. I. Title.

PS3562.A72 Z469 2000
813'.54,dc21
      [B]   00-044298

Distributed by Publishers Group West.

Designed by Pauline Neuwirth, Neuwirth & Associates, Inc.

Manufactured in the United States of America

My thanks to Amanda Urban, who brought the manuscript of this book to Nation Books. I also want to express my gratitude to Tom Engelhardt for his superior editing; to my daughter Kate, for moral and other support when I became ill and had difficulty working on the book; and to my son Jim, who under the same circumstances made an invaluable contribution to its final form and content.

—Ring Lardner, Jr.

introduction

Frances Chaney, Ring Lardner Jr.'s actress-wife doesn't believe
in speaking to informers. So one day in the mid-60s when Ring's old Hollywood
chum, the writer Budd Schulberg, encountered the Lardners at Sardi's restaurant,
he had to be nonplussed. While Frances turned her back on him, Ring, whom
Budd recruited into the Communist Party in the 1930s, and named as a
Communist before the House Committee on Un-American Activities (popularly
known as HUAC) in the 1950s, put out his hand and gave a friendly hello.

When I asked Lardner about this some years later he simply said, "I don't
believe in blacklisting." He is, one might say, recrimination-challenged and
this lack of bitterness or score-settling adds to the air of authenticity which
permeates this memoir of a modest man.

Ring Lardner, Jr., along with the late Dalton Trumbo, is probably the most
famous member of the original Hollywood Ten, also known as the "unfriendly
ten," who went to prison for contempt of Congress when they refused to answer
what was then known as the $64,000 question: "Are you now or have you ever
been a member of the Communist Party?" He is famous because of his epony-
mous father, the great American sportswriter and humorist, and for his films,
two of which won Academy Awards for best screenplay—the Katharine
Hepburn/Spencer Tracy vehicle Woman of the Year in 1942, and in 1970, after
fifteen years on the blacklist, M*A*S*H, the hilarious noir comedy about life
among the medics during the Korean War.

Introduction

But among the political cognoscenti he was most famous for the line which gives this book its title. One never knows what one would do if given the choice by an inquisitorial investigating Committee of either betraying one's beliefs and (former) comrades or losing one's livelihood. Lardner's response, for my money, met the Hemingway definition of courage, grace under pressure. As he told Committee Chair J. Parnell Thomas, "I could answer your question sir, but I would hate myself in the morning." Not since Ring Lardner, Sr.'s "Shut up, he explained" has there been a better line.

The Hollywood Ten collectively are important because they resisted McCarthyism at an historically critical moment before the Senator himself came on the scene. Their hearing was in 1947 and McCarthy made his famous Wheeling, Virginia speech about Communists in the state Department in 1951. Trumbo and Lardner also showed that it is possible to resist and prevail. At the time, of course, their action sent a very different message—that in the over-heated context of the domestic cold war, imprisonment could be the price one paid for exercising first amendment rights. (The Ten declined to answer HUAC's questions on First Amendment grounds, but most subsequent non-cooperating witnesses before HUAC and other congressional interrogators, learning from the Ten's example, invoked the Fifth Amendment's protection against self-incrimination and stayed out of jail, but not off the blacklist.)

Lardner calls his last chapter "Sole Survivor." And he is indeed the last of a family of four boys and a famous father; the last surviving member of the Hollywood Ten; and if not the "sole," he seems to be one of a handful of the survivors of an era in which people willing to go to prison for their beliefs were largely wiped out of social, cultural and political life—and so, in a sense, of our history. Much has been written of the Hemingway/Fitzgerald cohort who went to Europe in the 1920s as a "lost generation," but Lardner's memoir should remind us that he and his peers, not just the directors, screenwriters and other movie workers in Hollywood, but the librarians, teachers, scientists, defense workers, diplomats, union organizers and all those who lost out in the great red purge of the 1940s and 1950s were our real "lost generation."

The cultural costs of McCarthyism have never been, perhaps cannot be, computed. How do you count, no less put a political, cultural or even commercial value on plays and screenplays unwritten, careers not undertaken or cut off at birth, families and psyches smashed from the pressures of uncertainty compounded by the realities of unemployment? How to quantify the cost of inventions not invented, ideas not explored, hypotheses untested. Television itself was born, shaped and came of age in the context of McCarthy era assumptions, when a crazed grocer in Syracuse, who maintained a list of suspected Reds, held sway over prime-time employment decisions. Who is to say what contribution the great red scare made to the bland and timid television culture which prevails to this day?

Though these may not be the questions that preoccupy Ring Lardner, Jr. in this memoir, through it he offers us a very personal way to consider them anew. At the time he appeared in front of HUAC, he was gaveled down by J. Parnell Thomas before he could finish his statement. The full statement, printed in this book, is eloquent, but the book itself, this tale of life as a Hollywood communist offers the real answer to the Committee's question. That is the red meat, as it were, of a thoroughly unapologetic memoir by a man without many illusions.

Lardner makes clear that far from being glamorous, life as a Hollywood comrade was often time-consuming, boring and repetitious. Only occasionally did ideology enter the picture. Thus Lardner recommended to David O. Selznick that he not acquire Gone With the Wind "because I objected on political grounds to the glorification of slave owners and the Ku Klux Klan." Given the shortage of US Communists today, what is truly weird about this account of life just before, during and after the anti-Communist hysteria which dominated the political culture in the 1940s and 1950s, is its contemporary resonance. It is almost as if confronted with the absence of a 21st century Red Menace, a new generation of post-cold war would-be red baiters decided to rehabilitate the old one. These anti-anti-anti-communists—citing both a cache of recently released cables between Moscow and its agents in this country that were intercepted during World War II; and also selectively leaked documents from KGB archives—seem to argue that, in effect, McCarthy & Co. were right all along: That the new documents reveal that America did indeed suffer from an internal red menace, that Washington was a nest of spies, that those, like the late editor of The Nation, Carey McWilliams, who called the old congressional investigations a witchhunt, were either fools or knaves deploying a misleading or misinformed metaphor. There were no witches in Salem but there were indeed Communists in Washington.

No matter that there are a host of real, unresolved questions surrounding the new cache of cables (as deciphered they are incomplete, fragmentary, include false identifications, chronological discrepancies, internal inconsistencies, fail to distinguish witting from unwitting sources, to mention only some of the problems); no matter that the spin accompanying many of the newly "released" KGB documents turns out to be an updated version of the old McCarthy era equation: to be a liberal is to be a pinko is to be a communist is to be a spy; no

Introduction

matter that any fair reading of the new evidence suggests that it cuts more than one way and that the jury is still out on the role of the US Communist Party vis a vis Soviet espionage; no matter that although there were indeed live Communists on the American scene only an infinitesimal number of them may have deserved the demonized traitor/spy label. (Lardner, by the way, makes clear that there was undoubtedly espionage on both sides; indeed, he tried to serve in the OSS and wrote the script for a wartime movie starring Gary Cooper as an OSS agent.) The unseemly and ahistorical rush to reconvict the American left based on half-baked evidence, suggests the weakness of the new post-cold war red baiter's case, and reminds one of the political hysteria that is supposed to be part of our so-distant-as-to-seem-antique past.

Eventually HUAC was brought down by history, with a little help from the Yippies, building on the Lardner-Trumbo tradition of what Mark Twain once called "the assault of laughter." Jerry Rubin appeared before HUAC in a red Santa Claus suit. And Abbie Hoffman showed up for his testimony in a red, white, and blue T-shirt, duly ripped by unruly souvenir-hunting demonstrators and/or the cops. Asked by the judge if he would like to make a statement on his own behalf, he replied, "Yes, your honor. I regret that I have but one shirt to give for my country." By that time, 1968, it was possible to laugh HUAC and its roadshow out of town.

In this tragicomic memoir, full of fabulous Hollywood charm as well as political sadness, Lardner reports that he is often asked "Can it happen again?" His answer is, "Yes, but not in the same way." I would agree, and one of the reasons it can't happen in the same way is that Lardner, his buddy Trumbo, and a small platoon of other resisters over the years, made it so.

VICTOR NAVASKY

one In the Hot Seat

ON an autumn morning in Washington, in 1947, I appeared before the House Committee on Un-American Activities as an unwilling expert on the problem of "subversive influence in motion pictures." Presiding over the day's events was the committee chairman, Congressman J. Parnell Thomas of New Jersey. A former insurance salesman, Thomas was short and round and an aide had helpfully placed a telephone directory and a red silk pillow on his chair, thus putting him in full view of a chamber packed with reporters, photographers, radio commentators, newsreel crews, and spectators, and affording him physical parity, at least, with a publicity-conscious lineup of fellow probers who included the young Richard Nixon.

The committee counsel, the wan and clerical-looking Robert

Stripling, did most of the interrogating. But Thomas had a habit of taking over whenever he felt a witness was not being properly responsive, and that's how he felt, justifiably, at several points during my testimony.

"Aren't you a witness here?" Thomas demanded at last.

I acknowledged that I was, and our colloquy continued:

THOMAS

All right, then. A Congressional Committee is asking you: Are you a member of the Screen Writers Guild? Now you answer it yes or no.

ME

Well, I'm saying that in order to answer that—

THOMAS

All right, put the next question. Go to the sixty-four-dollar question.

ME

I haven't—

THOMAS

Go to the next question.

STRIPLING

Mr. Lardner, are you now or have you ever been a member of the Communist Party?

ME

Well, I would like to answer that question, too.

STRIPLING

Mr. Lardner, the charge has been made before this Committee
that the Screen Writers Guild which, according to the record, you
are a member of, has a number of individuals in it who are members of the Communist Party. This Committee is seeking to deter-
mine the extent of Communist infiltration in the Screen Writers
Guild and in other guilds within the motion picture industry.

ME

Yes.

STRIPLING

And certainly the question of whether or not you are a member
of the Communist Party is very pertinent. Now, are you a member or have you ever been a member of the Communist Party?

Reconstructing our encounter more than half-a-century later, I
have the congressional record to thank for the verbal details. It's
harder to recapture the mood that had seized the nation—its capital
in particular—so soon after the end of the global conflagration
known as World War II.

The war and the Depression, for all the suffering they caused, had
a tonic effect on many members of my generation. We had high
expectations of the postwar world. Victory over fascism had been
secured in the main by two great superpowers, one democratic, one
communist. They had found a way of working together for what we
took to be shared ideals, and the leaders of both nations now seemed
to realize that the introduction of atomic weapons made future wars
unthinkable. The case against racism and rabid nationalism had
been made in no uncertain terms, and in our own country, with the
New Deal, there had been a broad recognition of the need to soften

the impact of poverty and unemployment in the short run, and to bring about more equitable social and economic arrangements in the long run.

We were, as I said, young, and perhaps forgetful of the organized hatred and repression that radicals had faced in America as recently as the 1920s, when the authorities had locked up or deported countless suspected Reds and, on thin evidence, electrocuted Sacco and Vanzetti, who had the misfortune to be immigrants as well as anarchists. Since the thirties, not only current events but the personality and popularity of Franklin Roosevelt had kept the reactionaries and their sentiments in check. Now, scarcely two years after his death, FDR stood accused of "giving away" Eastern Europe at the Yalta Conference as though Washington had ever been in a position to control the destiny of a part of the world firmly occupied by the forces of the Soviet Union, which had pushed Hitler's army back to Berlin after suffering an estimated twenty million casualties in a counteroffensive that had done at least as much to win the war in Europe as the Allied invasion of France. (The same fanciful charge would soon be made about China.) Roosevelt's Democratic successor, Harry Truman, was quick to size up the Soviets as the postwar enemy. He responded by creating the C.I.A.; proclaiming a "Truman doctrine" to protect Greece and Turkey; playing hardball with our atomic-bomb monopoly; and instituting a loyalty-oath program that cost many federal workers their jobs. Still, in the eyes of the right-wingers, even Truman's loyalty was suspect.

One of the first acts of the Republicans who took control of Congress in 1946 (for the first time in twenty years) was to convert a temporary Committee on Un-American Activities, which had been investigating fascist sympathizers during the war, into a permanent one concentrating on the political left. The focus of the committee's first big "investigation" was the movie industry.

The notion of Hollywood as a fount of subversion may be difficult for some younger readers to comprehend. It was the heyday of the studio system, and my fellow witnesses and I worked for large commercial enterprises whose leaders were utterly dedicated to the free-enterprise system. Mostly Jewish immigrants from central and eastern Europe, they were self-made men, as the saying goes, and were inclined to wax sentimental about America as a land of opportunity. Their highest loyalty, second only to the flag, was entertainment.

In 1947, the studios gave us *Life With Father, The Ghost and Mrs. Muir,* and *The Bachelor and the Bobbysoxer.* My own contribution to that year's fare—a job not especially of my choosing—was the co-authorship of *Forever Amber,* a costume epic about a peasant girl who slept her way up and around in seventeenth-century England. The great social problem that my collaborator Philip Dunne and I tackled on that one was making an audience care whether Linda Darnell ended up with her true love, Cornel Wilde. (It was a challenge we failed to overcome. "You know what's wrong with this movie?" Phil said after an early screening. "It's the story of a resistible force up against a movable object.")

Our congressional inquisitors had much to say about a handful of sympathetic Hollywood treatments of life in Soviet Russia. But these were true curiosities made at the behest of the Roosevelt Administration in wartime when the U.S. and the Soviet Union had been allies. Louis B. Mayer could honestly describe M.G.M.'s contribution to the genre, *Song of Russia,* as "little more than a pleasant musical romance."

As screenwriters, which most of us were, our influence was limited; our political beliefs were, in any case, no less "American" than those of our inquisitors. Indeed, some of the views expressed by members of the committee in that period would seem obnoxious to most Americans today, as they did to us then. Congressman John

Rankin of Mississippi was given to racist and anti-Semitic rants like the one, delivered shortly after the hearing, in which he ticked off some of the names on a petition of support for us. His operatives had ascertained that June Havoc had been born June Hovick; that Danny Kaye's "real name" was David Daniel Kaminsky; that Eddie Cantor had once been Edward Isskowitz; and that Edward G. Robinson had gone by Emmanuel Goldenberger, among other revelations that Rankin described as "too numerous to mention."

Thomas and Nixon represented a more civilized form of witch-hunter, and the committee was now trying to distance itself from Rankin's harangues. Even so, the committee members and staff, like many of the studio executives, seemed to view the role that some of us had played in organizing the Screen Writers Guild and other motion picture unions as almost un-American in itself. We were also quizzed about our support in the thirties for the democratically elected government of Spain against the military revolt led by General Francisco Franco. "Premature anti-fascists" we had been labelled by, among others, F.B.I. director J. Edgar Hoover. At times, as in the interrogation of Bertolt Brecht on the same day I testified, even anti-government activity in Nazi Germany seemed to be worthy of exposure.

Most of us, in fact, belonged or had belonged to the Communist Party of the United States, but the meaning of that affiliation is very hard for people to grasp today, with all that has become clear about Communism as it unfolded in the Soviet Union, China, and other weak and impoverished nations over the course of the twentieth century. Neither I nor any of my friends in the party wanted the U.S. remodeled along Soviet lines. We deplored the absence of free elections, the cult of personality that surrounded Stalin, and the general atmosphere of regimentation. All these defects, though, we attributed to the lack of a democratic tradition in that country before the transition to socialism. In America, we believed, the conversion to a rational economic system would be accomplished peacefully at the polls. We also expected that under Marxist socialism, Russia would become more, rather than less, democratic, and the failure of that to happen was beginning to stir doubts among some of us even as we faced the committee.

In the scheme of revolutionary activities, ours had been, on the whole, rather temperate. Besides some educational sessions in Marxism, we had spent most of our party time organizing and strengthening the guilds and unions in the picture business. During the war, we had encouraged our colleagues and employers to do what they could to help bring about the defeat of Germany and Japan. What we did not do was act as spies for the Soviet Union. The Soviet government certainly had spies in America, just as the American government had spies in the Soviet Union. That's one of the things governments do: spy on each other. But about the dumbest thing a Soviet spy could have done—and the surest way to draw the attention of the F.B.I.—would have been to join the Communist Party of the United States.

In recalling that odd moment in American political history, however, I would be derelict if I did not also acknowledge that, defining subversion as they did, the committee's choice of Hollywood and its communist and left-liberal activists as a target was, on a certain rudimentary level, well-considered. Many of us had entered our professions with hopes, which we still harbored in varying degrees, that the great new medium of motion pictures would be a force for change, not in the crude way that such a thing might have been conceived in the Soviet world, but in the sense of allowing us to portray some of the not so beautiful realities of modern life and to gently illuminate areas of possible improvement.

As subject matter, both the depression and the war had brought out some of the best in Hollywood, and the movies had seemed to be coming down from the clouds, at least until Congress began looking our way. Fox, my employer, had in recent memory produced *The*

Grapes of Wrath and *How Green Was My Valley.* During an earlier stint at Metro-Goldwyn-Mayer, I had co-written the first of the Spencer Tracy/Katharine Hepburn films, *Woman of the Year,* in which Michael Kanin and I had tried to strike a modest blow for equality between the sexes. A subsequent script of mine, *Tomorrow the World,* had been a chance to show, through the story of a Nazi youth raised by American relatives, that racism and brutality, far from being the inherent traits of Germans or the Japanese, had to be learned and might therefore be unlearned.

Along with some of my Hollywood peers, I had hoped to see the studio system eventually yield to looser arrangements allowing even greater creative liberty. In 1945, I had been part of an effort to launch an independent production company focusing on documentaries and features about the kinds of social questions that the studios avoided. Even before the hearings, however, we had been forced to lower our sights as the studio bosses and their financial overlords in New York began to turn away from the "topical films" that, in any case, had never been more than a small part of their output. Still, to quote from a written statement that I carried onto the witness stand vainly hoping to be permitted to read it aloud, Hollywood was a "citadel of freedom" compared to Washington under the sway of the Committee on Un-American Activities.

"It seems to me you are trying to discredit the Screen Writers Guild through me," I replied to Thomas, "and the motion picture industry through the Screen Writers Guild, and our whole practice of free expression." I was about to add something about my understanding of the First Amendment when he interrupted again.

"Never mind your understanding," he fumed. "There is a question: Are you or have you ever been a member of the Communist Party?"

"I could answer exactly the way you want, Mr. Chairman," I replied.

"It is a very simple question," he continued. "Anybody would be proud to answer it—any real American would be proud to answer the question: Are you now or have you ever been a member of the Communist Party?—Any real American."

"It depends on the circumstances," I told him. "I could answer it, but if I did, I would hate myself in the morning."

With that sentiment, I had exhausted Thomas's patience. "Leave the witness chair," he commanded.

When I again protested my desire to testify, he pounded his gavel in exasperation. "Leave the witness chair!"

"I think I am leaving by force," I said.

"Sergeant, take the witness away!" he ordered. And the sergeant did so.

It was my first and, I had every reason to assume, my last encounter with Congressman Thomas. Three years later, however, we confronted each other as fellow inmates at the Federal Correctional Institution in Danbury, Connecticut, where I had been sentenced to one year for the misdemeanor of not answering his questions satisfactorily.

The blue prison fatigues hung loosely on the weary, perspiring man I met crossing the prison quadrangle. In the same costume, I felt that I looked comparatively dapper after eight hours of mild stenographic labor in the Office of Classification and Parole. Thomas's job as custodian of the chicken yard, while not exactly strenuous, had kept him in the August sun all day. He had lost a good deal of weight, and his face, smooth and scarlet at our last encounter, was now deeply lined and sallow, making him look ten years older. I recognized him, however, and he recognized me. We did not speak. How could either of us pick up where we left off? Since my conviction for Contempt of Congress, along with nine other Hollywood writers and directors, I had lost an appeal, and the Supreme Court had declined to review the constitutional issues in our case.

During the same period, Thomas had been brought to trial for putting nonexistent workers on the government payroll and appropriating their salaries for himself. Offering no defense and throwing himself on the mercy of the court, he had received a mild sentence, later reduced by parole to an actual term of about nine months—three months less than my own stint. When his case was due to be heard by the parole board, Thomas, I learned later, was worried that I might find some way to use my official capacity to sabotage his application. Actually, the case was taken out of my hands by a civilian clerk. Like the rest of my colleagues in the Hollywood Ten, I was denied parole. But I was the only one to receive, in addition to the statutory sixty days off for good behavior, an extra fifteen days for "meritorious good behavior." This was a reward for the improvements I had made in the grammar and style of the prison material I typed.

Though far from happy about my situation, it seemed more fluid than that of the sorry figure before me in the prison yard. Even if the torch of super-Americanism Thomas had brandished so fiercely during his two years of glory had not already been snatched from him by Senator Joseph McCarthy, there was no political future for a man whose downfall had been so pitilessly publicized and so prosaically self-aggrandizing.

My own future was at least unclear. I had taken the position that, while public servants are answerable to the people, private citizens cannot be summoned in the absence of even an allegation of an illegal act to account to the government for their beliefs and associations—matters that have traditionally been an American's own business. It was a First Amendment argument that commanded a good deal of support, some of it quite respectable. In fact, we had based our stand on the seemingly unequivocal language of a 1943 Supreme Court decision: "If there is any fixed star in our constitutional constellation, it is that no official, high or petty, can prescribe what shall be orthodox in politics, nationalism, religion or other matters of opinion, or force citizens to confess by word or act their faith therein."

Many people are surprised that the ten of us ended up not only blacklisted but imprisoned for refusing to discuss our political beliefs and associations. None of the hundreds later blacklisted in movies and television underwent the additional burden of being jail-birds. Ironically, in 1947, the Communist Party had not yet been deemed a criminal enterprise, and we were hardly eager to be the first to portray it in that light, as a plea based on the self-incrimina-tion clause of the Fifth Amendment might have implied.

By 1951, when the next hearings commenced, the leaders of the American Communist Party had been convicted under the Smith Act and were serving their sentences. (The statute in question made it a crime to advocate the forcible overthrow of the government. The party bosses were deemed to have done so not on the basis of any-thing they had said themselves, but on the indirect evidence of sen-timents expressed by Marx and Lenin as founding fathers of the movement.) So the Fifth Amendment had become a safe recourse— a way to avoid prison, at any rate—and once we had lost in the courts, there was no more point in citing the First. What witnesses couldn't avoid was the blacklist—unless they were willing to name names. I am not saying that we would have pled self-incrimination if we had been certain of our success. What seemed most important and urgent to us at that time was to put the committee out of busi-ness, and only a court victory on the freedom-of-speech issue seemed likely to accomplish that. After the resolution of our case, there was no reason for anyone else to take a position that had become so clearly self-defeating.

Subpoenaed by the Committee in 1952, Lillian Hellman composed a brilliant statement of her reasons for refusing to testify about others. "I am not willing, now or in the future . . . to hurt innocent people . . .

in order to save myself. . . . I cannot and will not cut my conscience to fit this year's fashions." Those were the words of a gifted writer, and they had an excellent propaganda effect against informing. But Lillian was also an instinctive dramatist, and she couldn't resist the opportunity to make her situation more suspenseful in her book *Scoundrel Time.* There she led readers to believe she had put herself in grave personal danger by insisting on the right to testify only about herself and not name other people. Some of the best legal minds in Washington, she wrote, felt that she was sending herself straight to jail by taking that position. In fact, she had made it clear in her letter to the Committee that if it failed to grant her the privilege she was requesting, she would simply invoke the Fifth Amendment on all questions. And by then, it had been established in case after case that there was no legal penalty for that. Just unemployment.

Within weeks of the first set of hearings, the heads of the movie studios met in New York and announced that none of us would work for any of them again until we had cleared ourselves with the Committee. Back in Hollywood, people went out of their way for us—a few to express their support, the majority to avoid our company. The talent guilds we had helped organize declined to support us, and soon passed new rules that made the blacklist easier to enforce. As it continued and expanded, some of us managed to work undercover at greatly reduced compensation; others had to find new occupations entirely; a few lost their lives in despair.

Nowhere else in the world, except possibly in the Kremlin, had there been a group of Communists with a higher standard of living or greater community acceptance than the writers who belonged to the party in Hollywood. One of the unwritten rules of membership, however, had been a polite understanding with our employers that we wouldn't advertise it. Now my colleagues and I—soon to be known as "The Hollywood Ten"—were a hot story, and the studio bosses could no longer engage in what today might be called a policy of "Don't ask, don't tell." Making my discomfort worse was my inability to simply refuse to answer the committee's questions and assert that my membership, in either the Communist Party or the Screen Writers Guild, was none of their business. But our lawyers, in an exercise of logic that seemed persuasive at the time, had insisted that such a stance could leave us vulnerable in court at a later date. We were instead supposed to maintain that we were making an attempt, in our own way, to answer the questions we felt the committee had no right to ask.

In recent decades, feelings in Hollywood, among other domains of American culture, have turned sharply in our favor. As the sole survivor of the Ten, I have been in a position lately to receive many expressions of respect and admiration from actors, actresses, and other denizens of the New Hollywood who sometimes have only a sketchy idea of what really happened to us. Since I enjoy a little adulation as much as the next man, I don't always make a point of filling in the gaps in their knowledge or correcting the points of confusion. But from time to time I try to suggest that we weren't as heroic as people make us out to be. It would be more analytically precise, it seems to me, to say that we did the only thing we could do under the circumstances, short of behaving like complete shits.

It's hard in the year 2000 to recall my thoughts as I sat on the witness stand. Like the others who testified with me, I couldn't yet know just how much liberty and property and comfort I was going to lose and for how long. None of the very tangible and personal consequences were clear to me as I leaned into the microphone, hoping only to be heard over the hubbub and to make a few telling points before the chairman cut me off. But I could begin to sense what has become more obvious with the years: The triumph of reason was going to take a little longer than I had imagined.

two
"I'm God, I think"

THE story of how I came to be a political prisoner goes back to my earliest years, when I displayed a compelling urge to shock people with unorthodox opinions, extravagant boasts, and wild exaggerations. At the breakfast table one morning when I was three, I threatened to commit mass murder. "If you say one more word to me," I announced, addressing my next older brother, Jim, "I'll kill you, Mr. Jimmie, and Mr. John [my eldest brother] and Mr. Daddy and Mr. Baby Brother."

To which Jim responded, "Oh, nobody could kill baby brother bees he's too little."

"I'll kill him because I'll bake him in the oven and kill him," I continued. "That's what I think I'll do."

Those were our exact words as set down by our father in his *Chicago Tribune* column, "In the Wake of the News," where he frequently described the family conversations at our house in Evanston and then, as we prepared to relocate to New York in the spring of 1919, in our apartment on Buena Avenue. We were moving east so that Dad, already known nationally for his *You Know Me Al* stories in *The Saturday Evening Post*, could write a syndicated column that would run in a hundred and fifty newspapers and make his one of the best-known names in America.

A skillful pianist and amateur songwriter, he was blessed with perfect pitch and an astonishing ability to render the way semiliterate Americans spoke and wrote. The combination of that remarkable ear and plentiful opportunities to listen to baseball players and other athletes as a sportswriter had produced a literary style all his own: "And he give her a look that you could pour on a waffle," says the cigar-salesman narrator of "The Big Town" about the man who has fallen for his sister-in-law. Elsewhere in the same collection of stories (which were, along with *You Know Me Al*, as close as my father came to writing a novel), we learn about a pricey hotel on Long Island where "They even got a barber and a valet, but you can't get a shave while he's pressing your clothes, so it's pretty near impossible for a man to look their best at the same time."

My father didn't want me named Ring and used his column to apologize for it:

> When you are nicknamed Ringworm by the humorists and
> wits,
> When people put about you till they drive you into fits.
> When funny folk say, "Ring, ring off," until they make you ill,
> Remember that your poor old Dad tried hard to name you Bill.

Having his name made me particularly aware of how well known it was. During his lifetime (he died in 1933 at the age of forty-eight) and for a considerable time afterward, the response I got when introduced was either, "You're related to the writer?" or "You're the writer?" But by the nineteen-forties and fifties, the recognition was beginning to fade, and eventually people started saying, "Ring? What kind of a name is that?"

An impressive-looking man, he had high cheekbones and deep-set eyes and stood two inches over six feet tall, which was unusual in his generation. He didn't talk a lot and almost never raised his voice, but what he had to say was always worth listening to and sometimes very funny—the more so because he didn't laugh as he was saying it. H.L. Mencken, Virginia Woolf, and Edmund Wilson, among others, saw him as a literary pioneer; nevertheless, Dad thought of himself primarily as a newspaperman, and it was his standards of journalism that he sought to pass on to his sons. With four New York papers delivered to the house every day, mealtime conversation was often about which one had handled a particular story best. Only my brother John had actually begun work as a reporter before Dad died, but the rest of us also got our first jobs on New York papers, and we all benefited from his instruction.

His continued insistence on identifying himself with journalism was part of a general refusal to take himself or his writing too seriously. "Are you a humorist?" I remember asking him when I was a child, based on something I had read.

"If I said 'yes' to that," he answered, "it would be like if somebody asked a ballplayer what position he played and he said 'I'm a great third baseman.'"

In 1924, when F. Scott Fitzgerald sold Max Perkins of Charles Scribner's Sons on the idea of a collection of Ring Lardner short stories,

Dad had no copies of most of them and couldn't remember where some had been published. After they had been dug out of various libraries and assembled, he accepted Scott's title, *How to Write Short Stories*. Instead of a serious introduction, though, he wrote: "A good many young writers make the mistake of enclosing a stamped, self-addressed envelope big enough for the manuscript to come back in. This is too much of a temptation to the editor. Personally I have found it a good scheme to not even sign my name to the story, and when I have got it sealed up in its envelope and stamped and addressed, I take it to some town where I don't live and mail it from there. The editor has no idea who wrote the story, so how can he send it back? He is in a quandary." Each story came with an explanation attached. "A Frame Up," actually about a boxing prodigy, was described as "a stirring romance of the Hundred Years War, detailing the adventures in France and Castile of a pair of well-bred weasels."

The year that first collection was published, my father offered his take on the European Dada movement, in the form of a play (never theatrically performed, to my knowledge) called *I Gaspiri*, or *The Upholsterers*:

ACT I

A public street in a bathroom. A man named Tupper has evidently just taken a bath. A man named Brindle is now taking a bath. A man named Newburn comes out of the faucet which has been left running. He exits through the exhaust. Two strangers to each other meet on the bath mat.

FIRST STRANGER

Where was you born?

SECOND STRANGER

Out of wedlock.

FIRST STRANGER

That's a mighty pretty country around there.

SECOND STRANGER

Are you married?

FIRST STRANGER

I don't know. There's a woman living with me, but I can't place her.

(Three outsiders named Klein go across the stage three times. They think they are in a public library. A woman's cough is heard offstage left.)

A NEW CHARACTER

Who is that cough?

TWO MOORS

That is my mother. She died a little while ago in a haphazard way.

A GREEK

And what a woman she was!

(The curtain is lowered for seven days to denote the passage of a week.)

The mind that could conceive such disjointed nonsense was the same one that prided itself on its accuracy in reporting factual events. In his account of a World Series game or a conversation among his sons, Dad was equally scrupulous in providing the reader with his best recollection of the acts and words he had witnessed. In these further excerpts from his Chicago columns, I am now three and a half and known as "Bill."

IN THE WAKE OF THE NEWS
BY RING W. LARDNER

CHARACTERS:

Le Père

La Mère

John, the eldest son

Jim, the middle-sized son

Bill, the son-of-a-gun.

SCENE: Breakfast

BILL

I'm all through with my breakus.

LA MÈRE

Have you got a kiss for me?

BILL

I can't be kissing people every day. Just Wednesday.

LA MÈRE

But this is Wednesday.

BILL

Just afternoons.

LE PÈRE

What kind of an automobile have you got, Mr. Bill?

BILL

I've got a dangerous automobile. It runs over big ladies.

JOHN

If you ran over ladies you'd get arrested.

BILL

It runs over policemen, too.

And in another installment:

BILL

But why didn't I get something?

LE PÈRE

You did, you got a ball, but it isn't your birthday. It's John's and Jim's birthday.

BILL

It is my birthday.

JIM

It isn't your birthday, bees you're not anything old.

I'd Hate Myself in the Morning

BILL

I am as old as you are, Mr. Jimmy.

JIM

You're not, bees I'm five years old.

BILL

I'm one billion and thirty-nine years old and that's old.

JIM

But you're not even older than John bees he's seven.

BILL

But I'm older than John because he's seven and I'm God. I'm older than anybody in the world. I'm the oldest man in the world, I think.

JIM

Oh, think yourself.

JOHN

If he thinks he's old, let him think he's old. We're older.

BILL

No, you're not, Mr. Johnny. Because I'm older than anybody.

JIM

Oh, older yourself. Giants are older.

BILL

I'm a giant myself. I'm God, I think.

Though the column ran seven days a week, Dad somehow found time to take on an array of other writing assignments, including a six-day-a-week comic strip of "You Know Me Al" and the script for a 1925 movie, *The New Klondike*, which involved a baseball player caught up in the Florida real-estate boom. (It was directed by Lewis Milestone, who would go on to make *All Quiet on the Western Front*.) By the mid-twenties, he had cut back on his newspaper work in order to concentrate on short stories. Even so, he managed to write revue sketches and song lyrics for Florenz Ziegfeld, contributing six numbers to the Ziegfeld–produced musical *Smile*, with a cast that included Fred and Adele Astaire. ("Someone gave me a rhyming dictionary for Christmas once," Dad told a reporter who wanted to know what had caused him to take up lyric-writing. "I couldn't exchange it for a tie.") A source of particular satisfaction to him, after a number of unsuccessful attempts to write for the stage, was the play *June Moon*, which he co-wrote with George S. Kaufman. A comedy about the popular songwriting business, it became one of the bigger hits of the 1929–30 Broadway season.

The excerpts quoted, along with later family revelations and my own memories, all testify to my impulse to assert myself. The fact that I was overweight and uncoordinated increased rather than diminished that need. The best way to get the attention I craved, it seemed, was to express opinions that ranged from the unexpected to the outrageous. By the time I was twelve, I had proceeded from iden-tifying with God to denying his existence. There was no such entity, I told a next-door neighbor. (Though his mother lodged a complaint with my mother, I am happy to say that the boy eventually recovered from the shock and became a Congressman.)

The most striking thing about our household was the absence of outward emotion. What we sought to express were our thoughts rather than our feelings. A raised voice was a rare and unwelcome event, and all of us were fairly adept at holding our tongues, though William Shawn, the longtime editor of the New Yorker, described my brother David, the youngest of us, as "a *little* more open and a *little* more talkative than the other Lardners . . ."

My brothers and I never had the traditional man-to-man talk about sex with our father. I doubt if he even considered it, since he would have been unable to say the necessary words. (They were quite literally unmentionable in our household.) Increasingly, in the last decade or so of his life, Dad realized that other people did speak them—indeed, that some writers found sex not only a permissible but a favorite subject. These peers, from his point of view, were unforgivably deficient in taste. In his own work, even as it grew deeper and more psychologically complex, there was never a suggestion of amorous passion; nor did he ever write anything that would normally be considered a love scene.

If roots in the New World were a defense, I would have been well-protected against the charge of Un-Americanness. Ancestors on both sides of my family had been here since the seventeenth century, and the Lardners as well as the Abbotts (my mother's forebears) were double pioneers, originally settling in Pennsylvania and Massachusetts, respectively, and then, in the mid-nineteenth century, in Michigan and Indiana. But their migration to the untamed Middle West is not to be confused with that of the propertyless pioneers in their covered wagons or the trainloads of European immigrants seeking free land— a hundred and sixty acres that, along with a lot of hard work, could support a family. The Lardners and Abbotts were looking for land, too, but in much larger quantities, as the best investment for their capital. As an added attraction, they were leaving metropolises with hundreds of upper-class people and heading for frontier settlements—Niles, Michigan and Goshen, Indiana—where they would share their elite status with no more than half-a-dozen other families.

Dad's maternal grandfather was rector of the Protestant Episcopal Church in Niles. My grandmother and aunt, both named Lena, played the organ in that church, consecutively, for a hundred and one years. The literalness of the religious faith of the older Lena can best be illustrated by a letter she wrote in 1898 to an acquaintance whose child had died:

> Dear Mrs. Miller:
>
> From my own experience I know how sad you are and how much you miss the bright child who was your sweet little companion in daily life. The only comfort for you is to try to realize that she is happy and safe. All that a loving mother could do for her does not compare with what her Heavenly Father has already done for her. After her brief suffering, she is safe and happy in His arms forever. It is by thinking of her joy that you can be consoled and with the Christian's faith, you look forward to meeting her again.
>
> Truly yours,
> Lena B. Lardner

There were people even in those days who would have found such a message of consolation infuriating in its smug righteousness, but we may assume my grandmother knew her recipient and that it was received in the same warmhearted spirit in which it was written.

My grandmother was Dad's only teacher until he was ten, when a private tutor took over his education and that of his two youngest siblings. So he was not subject to the kind of schoolyard talk, 1890s-style, through which children often gain some concept, however distorted, of the facts of life. He did, however, attend Niles High School for four years, and more significantly, after he became a sportswriter almost by accident, spent a decade in daily association with baseball players and other coarse creatures of the sporting world. Yet to a remarkable degree, he remained unaffected by these influences. As late as 1922, my brother Jim and I had our allowances canceled for a month for introducing the following sidesplitter at the dinner table:

Q: What was the longest slide in the Bible?
A: When Joshua went from Jericho to Jerusalem on his ass.

His old-fashioned values endured through the years that followed World War I, when styles of dress and speech as well as relationships between men and women altered so drastically. It didn't matter that the two fields with which he was most closely associated were sports and the Broadway theater, or that a favorite friend was Scott Fitzgerald, who wrote stories about the Jazz Age and dedicated a book of them (*All the Sad Young Men*) to Ring and Ellis, my parents.

Two decades earlier, they had conducted a long courtship mainly by correspondence. They didn't see much of each other because he was traveling most of the time with the Chicago White Sox or to other sporting events, while my mother, then Ellis Abbott, was an honor student at Smith College. After their formal engagement, she took a job teaching some of the faculty offspring at a military academy in Indiana, and he accepted one in St. Louis as editor of *The Sporting News*. His involved a raise from thirty-five to fifty dollars a week, but the main selling point he cited to Ellis and her family was that it would keep him in one place. After he quit that job, having discovered that his employer was a crook, he tried to sell Mr. Abbott on an offer he had received to become business manager of a minor-league baseball team in Louisville, Kentucky. But Ellis's father, she reported in one of her letters, "thinks a 'sporting man' is a 'sporting man' and can't change his spots, and that his daughters are delicate and rare things. And that they must not come in contact with that 'damned sporting crowd.'" Dad responded by addressing Mr. Abbott directly, promising him that "Ellis won't ever have to see a ballplayer or a ball game."

Then came a surprising twist. *The Boston American* offered him forty-five dollars a week to cover baseball there, and his future father-in-law raised no objection. To the Abbotts of Andover, evidently, an association with Boston made anything, even ballplayers, more refined. Interestingly, Dad never advanced as an argument in his favor the possibility that he might sell stories to magazines and so become a professional writer, maybe because he hadn't considered it. He was twenty-six when they were finally married in June 1911, and another three years passed before he wrote and sold his first piece of fiction to cover the expenses created by the arrival of his second son.

My mother was wise and charming as well as strikingly attractive, and we all derived as much from her as we did from our father. Besides the environmental influence, we got half our genes from the Abbott lineage. In all the important areas of parenthood, Mother and Dad shaped our attitudes. What they thought about books, art, music, theater, politics, people, and social behavior was what we responded to, usually affirmatively. With our father's encouragement, we followed the big sports events and the Broadway hits, while Mother inspired us to read Charles Dickens and Jane Austen, her favorite authors.

Raised in a Presbyterian household in Goshen, Indiana, where the rules of speech and conduct were pretty much the same as the Lardners's in Niles, Michigan, she was nonetheless better able to adjust to a changing environment. In her later years (she died in 1960), she could tolerate if not approve the idea of an unmarried couple living together. In his far shorter life, Dad never yielded any ground at all. Confined to a hospital most of the two years before he died (with his attitudes hardened, perhaps, by ill health), he listened to the radio and wrote reports on the new medium for *The New Yorker*, focusing on the sexually suggestive lyrics of popular songs. In his day as in ours, most writers were trying to break the bounds of censorship. By contrast, Dad was calling on the network censors to come out of hiding and cleanse the airwaves of such provocative lyrics as "As you desire me, So shall I come to you . . . Let come what may." Just on the borderline of acceptability, he wrote, was "Let's put out the lights and go to sleep." (Rumor had it, he told his readers, that "in the original lyric, the last word was not 'sleep.'")

His inflexible thinking about such things gave me a pretty accurate notion of turn-of-the-century standards in polite society. Now, at this new turn-of-the-century, when I note how those standards have altered, I find the change quite as drastic as the other great developments of the past hundred years. Each generation, of course, remarks on how much more freedom there is in speech, books, magazines, theater, and other media, and each generation seems convinced that permissiveness has gone about as far as it can go. Just a few years after my father's death, Cole Porter jokingly compared the "olden days," when "a glimpse of stocking was looked on as something shocking," with the licentiousness of 1936, when, "Heaven knows, Anything goes."

How would my father have reacted, I wonder, to the movies of the 1990s, with male and female frontal nudity, their almost obligatory intercourse scenes and, in dialogue, the forbidden word "fucking" as a leading modifier? Or to the recognition of gay and lesbian behavior as acceptable variations of sexual expression? During my early years in the movie business, the long list of words forbidden by the motion picture production code included floozie, trollop, tart, and at least a dozen other ways of describing a loose woman. There were also a large number of restrictions on what could be shown visually. These fell for the most part in two areas: first, explicit treatment of sex and certain designated parts of the human body; second, criminal acts or acts considered sinful unless the perpetrators were duly punished for them, usually by death. The cause of death, incidentally, could be completely unrelated to the offense. It was okay for a character to get away with robbery, murder, or adultery—with almost any offense imaginable, in fact, as long as you tacked on a scene later in the story in which he met a terrible end in an earthquake or some other chance disaster.

These days, characters are no longer required to do penance for their misdeeds, and there is no word that cannot be spoken on the screen. *M*A*S*H*, in 1970, was the first major American movie in which the word "fuck" was spoken. Although the script was mine, it was Bob Altman, the director, who added the expletive. After the picture received an "X" rating from the censors, the studio executives decided to fight it. In the end, they succeeded in winning an upgrade (or downgrade, depending on your perspective) to an "R." Things have grown even more permissive between then and now, and you might be tempted to conclude, on the basis of recent releases, that there is nothing that cannot be shown on the screen today. Based on the record of the twentieth century, however, it is probably safer not to predict what will be allowed in the twenty-first.

Fame and its rewards affected us profoundly. The house we moved into in the East was a large one on a hill in Great Neck, Long Island. There was a series of terraces in front and artificial levels behind that dropped gracefully toward the waters of Manhasset Bay. The first of these, our mother's territory, was a more or less formal flower garden with a circular lawn and a goldfish pool. The next contained a three-car garage, stables, and a vegetable garden. Then came a tennis court, which on a few choice winter nights could be flooded and converted into a hockey rink, and finally the largest level of all, accomodating a full-scale playground with an elaborate set of gymnastic equipment and a baseball diamond big enough for Little League play.

Two strong forces encouraged us to use these facilities to their fullest. There was Dad, a firm believer in the interdependence of a healthy mind and healthy body; and there was Miss Feldman, our Prussian-born, uniformed, trained nurse, who was even more partisan on the subject. Added to the familial entourage after my youngest brother David's birth in 1919, she had come home from the hospital with Mother. Her then-comfortable live-in salary was seven dollars a day for as much time as she was needed, which turned out to be ten of the next twelve years.

Most employees try to limit the scope of their responsibilities; Miss Feldman only strove to increase hers. Her supervision became an increasingly dominant factor in our lives, more so than our parents realized because it was in her nature to move inexorably into any vacuum. Such vacuums were created in the main by two strong drives of Mother's. One was to be with other people—to entertain and be entertained, to keep abreast of books and the theater, and to fill her guest bedrooms with as many Lardners and Abbotts and unrelated visitors as she could possibly coax into them. The other impulse (often in conflict with the first) was to be the most helpful wife she could be to an ever more famous man, assuming the roles of social secretary, business agent, and protector against his many admirers and his inclination to do favors for relatives and friends. These duties expanded steadily as his health and his resistance to alcohol declined.

The passage of time has not fully vindicated Miss Feldman's approach to child-raising. Besides providing us with a diet packed with cholesterol and rigidly supervising our toilet visits, she was obsessed with the benefits of fresh air. The third floor of our house was occupied by servants, generally three of them, among whom Miss Feldman, as she frequently reminded us, was not one. The six bedrooms on the second floor should have been more than a reasonable number for seven people, but not the way they were actually allocated. Dad and Mother, at her insistence because of his drinking and working habits, each had a room; so did Miss Feldman, and there were two guest rooms. That left one room for the boys, but it didn't even have a single bed in it; we used it as a dressing room. The four of us spent our nights, including the ones when we froze the tennis court, sleeping on a screened porch with awnings that could be lowered against anticipated precipitation. The unanticipated kind made its way through the screens with considerable freedom. I can recall lying awake while an inch of snow accumulated on the floor. Each of us waited in silence for a more enterprising brother to get out of bed and let down the awnings.

After entering the house to dress and have breakfast, we would be dispatched to the playground until the time came to leave for school. John, from the age of nine on, was regularly driven to a private school in a neighboring community and picked up daily by our current chauffeur-gardener. Jim and I, and eventually David, were transported in the other car to a different, expensive private school by Miss Feldman, relentlessly dressed in a white, starched uniform and matching nurse's cap. Mother, who had driven during the first two years of her marriage, never took the wheel after a Chandler, with the standard soft-top of the day, overturned and John, then a baby, was thrown out unhurt. It was at Dad's request that she gave up driving.

While all the other children had lunch at school, Miss Feldman, more days than not, arrived in uniform and cap to whisk us off to the superior fare she provided at home, and then, if there was time, to our private playground, before returning us to the afternoon session. The school day usually wound up with athletics outdoors: the colder the winter weather, the better the hockey on the school pond. Even so, we were invariably dispatched to the playground upon our return home. For roughly the duration of Daylight Savings Time, that was also where we went after supper until darkness impended. As for summer vacation, I doubt if we ever averaged more than two hours out of twenty-four indoors on a rainless day.

Our father didn't communicate much with Miss Feldman directly, but when it came to exercise they were very much on the same wavelength. His own upbringing had been deplorably soft, he believed, and he didn't want us to carry the same burden of indolence. One summer, he went as far as to hire an All-American end from Vanderbilt University to teach us basic gridiron skills. We devoted two days a week to our football studies for about a month, without any promising results. Jim, the only one of us with speed and agility, was too light for football, never reaching a hundred and fifty pounds. The other three of us were simply not the stuff of which athletes are made, and in this respect I was outstanding. Consistently overweight until my mid-twenties, I was also physically inept.

We certainly made use of the tennis court, the beach and, when we could gather enough visiting cousins or schoolmates, the baseball diamond. The start of one such game was briefly delayed when a visiting player noticed an unusual design on the ball and found, on closer examination, that it had been autographed by the entire New York Yankee team including Babe Ruth and Lou Gehrig. We loftily informed him that we always played with autographed balls, replenishing our supply whenever we visited a ballpark and the players came over to greet Dad and offer us their standard gifts. It was the one piece of sports equipment he didn't have to pay for.

But the great majority of our outdoor hours were spent reading—

horizontally, as a rule, perhaps because we inherited the nearsightedness of the Abbotts. At any given moment, two or three of us might be stretched out on the ground with a book. For days when the ground was too damp or too cold, there was a swing with two facing seats and a capacity of four. I have never found a better test of an author's grip on my attention than reading in that swing on a really cold winter day. Dumas was the most dangerous, especially the *Count of Monte Cristo* and *The Vicomte de Bragelonne*. (Who decided that one name should be translated, the other not?) His novels so engrossed me that I'd forget to stamp my feet occasionally to ward off frostbite.

Did we become readers by inheritance or acquire the habit by imitation? Dad always had a book in hand, but the amount of time he gave to reading kept diminishing. His favorite author was Dostoevsky; his favorite book, read many times, *The Brothers Karamazov*. In the last years of his life, however, he rarely read fiction, opting instead for one book after another about the American Civil War. Mother, then and always the only college graduate in the family, spent about the same amount of time revisiting the classics as she did covering current fiction. Among the children, it was a matter of course that you were able to read and write by the age of four, and by six it was practically a full-time occupation. (We all began to wear glasses in our teens.) In first grade, I was detached from my peers and assigned to the third grade for reading purposes only. We each skipped a grade at one point or another, though David required special coaching for the purpose. His tutors were Jim and I, at ten cents an hour apiece.

If any considerable part of the reading and writing we did at home had been devoted to schoolwork, we would have been prize students. Regrettably, homework had a low priority among us. Our report cards fell into a predictable pattern: high marks in English and one or two other subjects we liked, just getting by in the rest. The lowest marks were likely to be for "effort." Jim was the only one who shared Mother's facility for mathematics, which, along with his English skills, kept his grades above the family norm until his first year at Harvard, which he devoted to songwriting.

I was regarded as the difficult one in the family and invariably got myself into the most trouble, out of a spirit of undirected rebelliousness. Perhaps some of that was a defensive reaction to having brothers one and three years older. If I felt put upon, and I did, the forces that united, in kindergarten and at home, to correct my natural left-handedness by instructing me to write and eat right-handedly only compounded the problem. Undoubtedly, this explains the scrawl I'm left with instead of respectable handwriting. My junior position in the hierarchy probably also contributed to a stutter that plagued me intermittently until boarding school, when I deliberately went in for public speaking and whittled the problem down to a mere speech hesitation.

Jim and I, only fifteen months apart in age, were a sharp contrast physically. I grew to six feet and at one time over two hundred pounds. He was slight though remarkably strong. He played rugby and lacrosse in college and became a New England intercollegiate wrestling champion, incidentally mastering the technique of tearing a Manhattan phone book in half. His mental processes were superbly logical, and I never saw him, as boy or man, display anger or more than the mildest sort of enthusiasm for anyone or anything. Some observers have noted similar mental and emotional patterns in me, but they're a pale imitation of his.

Despite our differences, Jim and I found ourselves in splendid accord most of the time. We liked the same books, games, movies, radio programs, and people. We had an appreciation of, and sensitivity to, each other's minds that enabled us to divine in most situations what the other was thinking. This paid off for us financially when we partnered at bridge.

None of the four of us was ever enrolled in a public institution of any kind. When we completed eighth grade, the local high school was not even seriously considered. I didn't question this policy at the time, and I thoroughly enjoyed my four years of boarding school at Phillips Academy in Andover, Massachusetts, the town where the Abbott family had settled in the seventeenth century. By the time my own children were ready for high school, however, I had developed a strong preference for public education. Happily, this evolution in my thinking coincided with a sharp drop in income as a result of the blacklist.

My educational biases sprang partly from the recollection of an American history class at our Great Neck grade school. My classmates, of whom there were never more than seven or eight, were the children of investment bankers, corporate presidents, and the like. Adapting herself splendidly to her audience, our teacher presented us with the heroic struggle of Theodore Roosevelt against the temptations of wealth and idleness. It was no big deal, she maintained, to work hard and make a name for yourself if you were born in a log cabin and you didn't have any other choice. But when the heir to a proud name and a secure fortune dedicated himself to public service, it was sheer altruism all the way.

In 1928, our parents sold the house in Great Neck and moved to East Hampton at the other end of Long Island. In those days it was still a small town bordering the fishing village of Amagansett. A few socialite families and a smaller number of artists and writers had summer places there. My parents had joined with their closest friends, the sportswriter Grantland Rice and his wife Kate, in buying beach property and building adjoining houses on the dunes. Where the joint driveway separated, Dad had a sign made that said

"Dixie Highway" and pointed toward the Rices, who came from Tennessee and Georgia respectively. The year of their move was also the year I joined John and Jim at Andover, so the beach house, where we spent our summers, was the only home we had from then on. During the shorter Christmas and spring vacations from school and college, we had temporary quarters in Manhattan, where our parents and David lived eight months a year while he attended a private day school.

The main attractions of East Hampton for the four of us were the twenty-one grass tennis courts at the posh Maidstone Club and swimming in the breaking waves of the open Atlantic. We made a special point of going into those waves on the days the Coast Guard raised a red flag signaling that they were too rough for swimming.

In a poll of the two hundred boys in Andover's class of 1932, I was not ranked in the categories Most Respected, Most Capable, Most Promising, Most Popular, or Best Student, but I took first place in Most Original, Wittiest, and Biggest Bluffer in Classroom; I came in second in Laziest, Windiest, and Hardest to Rattle. But my reputation among the classmates who knew me best rested on a series of entertaining campaigns against what I considered objectionable school practices and regulations.

There was a daily chapel service conducted by the headmaster, and on Sundays both a morning and evening service conducted by a guest clergyman. The morning ones tended to be quite lengthy and I chose to call attention to that fact one Sunday by putting an alarm clock in the drawer of the lectern, set to go off twenty minutes after the visiting preacher began to speak. By a happy accident, the drawer stuck closed, and the alarm continued to ring until it ran down.

Permission to smoke was granted to seniors only in one special designated area. I deliberately arranged to be seen with a pipe in my mouth by a particularly officious faculty member on a campus path that was not so privileged. It was a cold winter day, and the illusion that I was violating the rules was greatly enhanced by the fact that the air I exhaled resembled smoke. It was a pleasure to demonstrate to him that the pipe was empty and his was a false accusation.

There were Greek-letter clubs at Andover, imitations of college fraternities, and some of them made themselves especially sacrosanct by barring non-members from ever entering their premises. I led a nocturnal foray into one of these, leaving behind evidence that anonymous visitors had violated the shrine. If the perpetrators of a stunt like that had been discovered, we would have been placed on probation. I was also involved several times in offenses that could have resulted in instant expulsion. The Prohibition Amendment was in force at the time and speakeasies, being illegal, naturally didn't require proof of age. I was one of a small group of venturesome boys who would sneak out of our dormitories on a Saturday night, board a bus to the nearby industrial town of Lawrence, and spend an hour or two drinking bootleg beer.

The most memorable event of my years at Andover was my four-story fall from a dormitory window ledge. I was standing on that narrow ledge holding onto a shutter because I intended to enter by window the locked room of a boy who had refused to share a box of goodies from home. I had my advance foot on his ledge when the shutter came loose, and I lost my grip, falling to a patch of lawn and fracturing my shoulder and pelvis. (My head missed a cement block by about six inches.) I spent the next six weeks in the school infirmary and a Boston hospital. Despite all this activity and inactivity, I managed to function as editor of the school literary magazine and to graduate with a decent academic record while garnering prizes for writing and speaking at commencement, where I also served as class historian.

The first political stand I can remember taking was to declare

myself a Democrat in the early stages of the Great Depression, partly because I found the image of President Herbert Hoover displeas-
ing and partly to annoy my parents, who were nominal Republicans,
although they rarely bothered to vote. I had not yet turned sixteen
when, at a bus stop between Boston and New York in June of 1931,
I climbed onto the roof of the vehicle in which Jim and I were traveling home from Andover, and—at no one's urging but my own—
delivered an impromptu speech in support of New York Governor
and presidential candidate Franklin Delano Roosevelt.

But by November, had I been eligible to vote for him, I would
not have done so. I was spending my weekends touring the state of
New Jersey as a member of the Socialist Club of Princeton
University, and mounting soapboxes to further the candidacy of
Norman Thomas, Class of 1905, who returned to the campus twice
a year to preach at a Sunday chapel service and meet in the
evening with his political disciples in the student body. I can't
recall all the factors that led me to this conversion; certainly, one
was the congressional candidacy on the Socialist ticket in
Connecticut of Heywood Broun, a friend of my father's who always
gave us boys something to think about and laugh at. But he would-
n't have had such an influence on me, I'm sure, if not for the bigger factor in my leftward migration: the growing severity of the
Depression and what I assessed as the failure of both major parties
to come to grips with it in their platforms.

The idea of going to Princeton originated with another family
friend, Scott Fitzgerald, who described its virtues to me when I was
about eight. My brothers and I liked Scott, who told us stories and
performed card tricks for us. But it was Zelda, his wife, who made
the greater impression on me at that age. I have never seen a photograph that conveyed the beauty I saw in her, or known another adult
who seemed to say whatever came into her head without any dis-

cernible exercise of judgment.

Scott and Zelda moved to France after only a year and a half as neighbors of ours. During the Great Neck period, the friendship that developed between Dad and Scott was based in part on their joint fondness for alcohol. They were nearly twelve years apart in age and drastically different in ambitions and opinions, but they so enjoyed each other (and the whiskey) that they sometimes talked all night and needed a day or more to sleep it off before they could get back to work. Scott was a great conversationalist in those days, vain but charming, full of ambition and concern about his literary reputation. Dad was also captivated by Zelda, whose symptoms of mental illness were not yet manifest. "Mr. Fitzgerald is a novelist," he once wrote, "and Mrs. Fitzgerald is a novelty."

Four years later, in 1937, I met a far different Scott at Dorothy Parker's house in Hollywood, and saw him intermittently until his death in December 1940. In the intervening period, as described in his book *The Crack-up*, he had undergone a drastic personality transformation. He spoke little and without visible emotion, and he was able to stay on the wagon for longer stretches of time. But when he went off it, recovery was a much harder struggle. He was pessimistic about the movie work he was doing and about what had happened to his standing as a writer. He had to face the fact that his books were no longer selling, while his former protégée, Ernest Hemingway, had a smash hit in *For Whom the Bell Tolls*. Scott died without finishing his final novel, *The Last Tycoon*, and without any grounds for anticipating that he would come to be regarded as a literary pioneer and one of the great American writers of the century.

A classmate who became a close friend and my roommate my sophomore year was Herbert Bayard Swope, Jr., whose family had also lived nearby in Great Neck. Swope, Sr., had been editor of the highly regarded *New York World*, and I spent a good deal of weekend time at their family homes in Manhattan and Sands Point, Long Island, which were known as gathering places for the cream of New York literary society. One of the people I met through the Swopes was Alexander Woollcott, the dramatic and literary critic, essayist and radio star-to-be, who engineered my first professional writing assignment at the age of seventeen.

Launching a new magazine called *Esquire* in the spring of 1933, the editor Arnold Gingrich decided to commission an article from a representative of the college generation. Woollcott recommended me, having read my work in Princeton's literary and humor magazines, and I eagerly accepted. It didn't occur to them or me that it might be inappropriate, even arrogant, for a freshman with less than six months of campus experience to undertake such an assignment. ("Good God," my father said when he saw my "Princeton Panorama" in the inaugural issue of the magazine. "Isn't any one of you going to turn out to be anything but a writer?") My story was advertised on the cover alongside the work of Hemingway, Dashiell Hammett, John Dos Passos, and Erskine Caldwell. I was the only one of these luminaries, in fact, to receive a full-page photographic portrait. In the piece itself, I maintained that college was more important as a social experience—a place to make "contacts" and join in "bull sessions"—than for any knowledge to be acquired by the conventional academic means. I described Princeton as "one of the oldest and most refined gentlemen's finishing schools in the country" and noted that "the curriculum is one of the best furnished in an American college, and is adequate for any gentleman." A number of people commented favorably on my contribution, and I scarcely noticed that none of them was a Princeton upperclassman. After all, I hardly knew any Princeton upperclassmen.

three
The Family Curse

I was about to leave East Hampton for my sophomore year at Princeton when Mother asked me to wait a while. She was worried about Dad's condition, and I was the only other family member at home. David had departed for Andover and Jim for Harvard. John, after a year at Harvard and a year at the Sorbonne in Paris, was living in the city and working as a reporter for the *Herald Tribune*.

The last couple of years had not been good ones for my father. He had developed tuberculosis and a mounting inability to go on the wagon without confining himself to a hospital. The immediate cause of his death, at age forty-eight, was a heart attack. It was not until John died of the same cause at forty-seven that I had my first cholesterol test with its alarming count in the 400s and learned that the

gene for super-high accumulations of the stuff was in the Lardner
DNA. John's son, one of my sons and a grandson were all later found
to have dangerously high counts. The four of us have been surviving
ever since on strong medication.

Alcohol had also played a significant part in Dad's decline, and
he had been conscious of its ill effects for years. Prior to the enact-
ment of Prohibition, he had even briefly entertained the hope that
such a law, regardless of its general soundness and consequences,
might be a help to him personally in kicking the habit. In the event,
however, he and his friends Grantland Rice and Rube Goldberg, who
happened to be in Toledo, Ohio, to see Jess Willard fight Jack
Dempsey when the reform took effect, were quick to investigate the
new phenomenon of illegal liquor, and happy to learn that it wasn't
so very different, biochemically, from the legal kind. Later he
expressed his considered view of the great experiment in
"Prohibition Blues," a song that became the standout hit of a femi-
nist musical called *Ladies First,* starring the popular Nora Bayes.

> *I've had news that's bad news*
> *about my best pal*
> *His name is Old Man Alcohol*
> *but I call him Al . . .*

Like many alcoholics, his efforts to stop drinking never lasted
long. In at least one important respect, though, his case was pecu-
liar. Others sought and found in liquor a release from their inhibi-
tions about using rough language or making sexual advances. Not
Dad. He had an idealized concept of marriage that made his drinking habits seem incompatible with wedded bliss. His courtship letters took it for granted that he would not drink after marriage. In
practice, he switched from a pattern of regular daily drinking to

alternating periods of abstinence and indulgence, with the latter growing steadily more intense and long-lasting as the years passed.

Mother had realized for some time that he was a dying man and that there wasn't much she could do about it. Still, she applied all her strength and endurance to the effort, and her grief when it failed was overwhelming because he had become her main purpose in life. She was just beginning to revive her other ties to the world when, five years later, Jim was killed in the Spanish Civil War.

While no more than one in ten Americans is an alcoholic, among twentieth-century writers the proportion rises to something like one in three. Without much effort, I can summon the names of Eugene O'Neill, William Faulkner, James Thurber, Dorothy Parker, John Cheever, John O'Hara, Tennessee Williams, Ernest Hemingway, John Steinbeck, Raymond Chandler, Robert Benchley, Dashiell Hammett, Theodore Dreiser, Sherwood Anderson, Edna St. Vincent Millay, and—the first two drunks I knew and could identify as such—Sinclair Lewis and Scott Fitzgerald. Each of them in the course of an evening at our house would become, visibly and volubly, a far less attractive person. As a child, I was not aware of any similar alteration in my father's behavior; he was noted for maintaining physical control despite considerable consumption of alcohol, and he was particularly careful in the presence of his sons. For most of his binges, he went into New York and stayed at a hotel or club. Since this was also his practice when meeting a story deadline, we had no way of distinguishing between the two. I was well into my teens before I realized that he was an alcoholic, and by that time the episodes were occurring less and less often in the face of debilitating disease and hospitalization.

There has been a lot of speculation about what makes writers become drinkers (or the other way around). Life has put me in a position to discuss this topic with some authority, and I can lend my support to a few of the standard theories: the stress of deadlines, the search for answers to difficult creative problems, the need to face internal demons on a regular professional basis. Another explanation, easily overlooked, is opportunity. If you work in a public place, as most people do, it's difficult to go off on a bat; practical considerations force you to postpone your drinking until the working day has ended. Writers, who set their own hours of labor and diversion from labor, have an easier time sustaining a career and an addiction—for a while.

Literary critics and others have wondered about the roots of the despair that presumably provoked my father to start drinking again despite his awareness of the addiction. My prolonged empirical research into the same disease leads me to conclude that drinking is more apt to increase depression than relieve it. The alcoholic is distressed by his failure to conquer the addiction; hoping to ease his distress, he turns to drinking, which has an effect opposite to the one intended. This vicious circle was aggravated in my father's case by a puritanical conscience.

Watching his death happen was the first major emotional event that I can recall. But it didn't take the form of a sudden shock. There was no surprise, just the realization that a highly-prized and dearly-loved element of my life had been taken away. After completing the cremation arrangements and taking stock of a tremendous volume of mail and cables from all over the world, we moved Mother into New York, where John would be nearby, and I headed back to college.

Catching up with my studies was far from my first priority, however. The big question confronting me on my arrival, a week late, was whether I felt up to working on Princeton's annual Triangle Club show. In a competition held the previous spring, I had been chosen to collaborate on the script with a senior; I would be the first sophomore so honored. Without hesitation, either on family or academic grounds, I declared my readiness to proceed, although I knew I would have to put most of my energy into writing and rehearsing in order to put the show on in Princeton and New York before Christmas.

It was 1933, well before the era of co-education, and our chorus "girls" were female impersonators. Otherwise, the production attained a fairly high amateur level. The previous year's star, Jose Ferrer—now a graduate student of architecture—dropped in to share his insights with the director, Dr. Donald Stuart, a middle-aged professor of French. "Joe, do you think that's dirty?" Dr. Stuart asked worriedly, about a scene underway onstage. "No," the younger man replied, "but I'll show you how you can make it dirty."

I completed my sophomore year in June of 1934, a few months shy of my nineteenth birthday. Besides the Triangle show, I had written a monthly column for the *Princeton Tiger* called "Under the Table with Ring Lardner, Jr.," and I had represented the university on bridge and debating teams. The fact that I had made some kind of mark, at least socially, was indicated two years later in the yearbook of the graduating Class of 1936. Amid photographs and membership lists of all the standard extracurricular organizations was a page with a photo of several of my classmates and the unexplained initials "L.O.L.A." Unknown probably to anyone but them and me, the letters stood for "Loyal Order of Lardner Admirers."

What I clearly had not achieved was any record of academic accomplishment or any other benefits sufficient, by my reckoning, to justify the drain on Mother's reduced income as a result of Dad's death. John and Jim had already dropped out of Harvard. Now she acceded reluctantly to my decision as she had to theirs (and would later to David's to leave Yale). In my case, she squeezed five hundred dollars out of her budget for a summer in Europe before I embarked on a career. I arranged cheap steamer passage on the

Hamburg-Amerika Line, which many people were boycotting because of Hitler's accession to power, and a tour of the Soviet Union at the lowest Intourist rate of five dollars a day, which was to cover travel, hotel, and meals.

A few days in Hamburg and Berlin and, on my way back from Russia, three weeks in Munich left me with a highly unfavorable impression of the New Germany. In Munich, I stayed with an architect's family, getting into a number of debates with one of the young men of the househould, who was a member of the Hitler Youth Corps. "We really have nothing against the Jews," he assured me. Nothing, he went on to say, except their disproportionate representation in the ranks of lawyers and doctors. A fairly polished and cerebral spokesman for the new order, he gave the Jews credit for intelligence and hard work, and lamented that many Germans were not as industrious. But the bottom line of his analysis—the point that struck me, anyway—was his relentless need to distinguish between Germans and Jews. That the one could not also be the other seemed to go without saying.

My reaction to Soviet Russia, on the other hand, was enthusiastic. My own country was paralyzed by unemployment, want, and fear. Western Europe was stricken by the same miseries. In Russia, I saw construction everywhere and planning for the future on a grand scale. Despite the language barrier, the feeling I got, even from people seriously deprived by American standards, was one of hope and optimism at a time when most of the world seemed to be bogged down in stagnation and gloom or, like Germany, marching ardently backward toward barbarism.

It may come as a surprise to modern readers that in those days Socialism and Communism were associated with new, radical trends in social behavior, sexual relations, and art. This had begun to change under Stalin, and in the two subsequent decades of his dictatorship, would wither into the moral and social rigidity that lasted right up to the collapse of the Soviet Union. But one manifestation of the revolutionary spirit that still survived in 1934 (and was certain to strike an eighteen-year-old American boy as radical indeed) involved swimming along the Moscow River. The waterfront was segregated into four separate, fenced-off beaches: male nude, female nude, mixed in bathing suits, and mixed nude.

In a matter of months after America's belated recognition of the Soviet Union, the University of Moscow had established an Anglo-American Institute for English-speaking students. One of them was the former president of the Socialist Club at Princeton. I called on him the day I reached Moscow. The next day, I canceled the rest of my program with Intourist, moved into a dormitory at the university and enrolled myself in Sociology II or "Crime and Punishment in the Soviet Union."

The Americans at the Institute had gone to Russia, for the most part, under the aegis of the decidedly left-wing National Students Union. Two members of the Dartmouth delegation were to be among my closest friends in Hollywood, Budd Schulberg and Maurice Rapf, both sons of important movie executives. Two and a half years later, Budd and I were a writing team for David Selznick. Maurice went on to teach film at Dartmouth, where, as a student in the early thirties, he was a founder of the film society.

Of the three of us, Budd was the most ideologically committed. I was viewed, by contrast, as something of a rightwinger. I nearly got thrown out of the country, in fact, for a frivolous deed that I committed in cahoots with a Canadian student named Mark. A group of our peers had put up a "wall newspaper" whose leaden seriousness prompted the two of us to post one of our own. Our comic intent was, we believed, unmistakeable, so we were ill-prepared for the reaction of one Professor Pinkevich, a robust scholar with bushy eyebrows who had been selected to run the Institute despite his flimsy command of English. Summoned to a meeting called for the purpose of critiquing our work, we found that he had provided himself with an interpreter in order to prevent misunderstanding. As Mark and I entered the room, Pinkevich rose and greeted us formally. Then he sat down again while the interpreter opened the proceedings:

"Gentlemen, this is a very serious matter. The professor desires me to inform you that it was he who removed your wall newspaper from the bulletin board. He did so in his official capacity as director of the Institute. He did so for the reason that, in any Russian institution there can be only one wall newspaper, and that is the one that is sanctioned by the authorities. Secondly, and the professor believes this is more important, you have made fun of certain people and certain institutions, which it does not seem proper that you as guests of the Soviet Union should do."

"It is not proper that guests of the Soviet Union should do this," the professor put in.

"May I speak?" Mark asked.

"What?" said the professor.

The interpreter repeated the question in Russian.

"Da, Da, most certainly. That is what we are here for."

"We had no idea that it was a crime—"

"No, no, not a crime," the interpreter said hastily.

"Certainly not," said the professor.

"Well, we had no idea it was against the rules to put out an independent newspaper. You see, I come from Canada, and he comes from the United States, where we have freedom of the press."

"Freedom of the press?" said the professor. He spoke with the interpreter in Russian.

"The professor wishes me to say that in no country in the world is there more freedom of the press than there is in Russia. Here the press belongs to the people."

"But everything must be permitted by the official," the professor added.

"As you say," I put in, "the main point is whether we have ridiculed things which you hold sacred. It seems to me you must have misunderstood what we wrote. We certainly didn't mean anything counterrevolutionary."

"Counterrevolutionary? Oh, no," said the interpreter,

"Certainly not," said the professor.

"If you would point out the passages to which you object," I suggested.

After they had consulted for a few minutes, the professor produced an article torn from our short-lived effort. The interpreter glanced through it. "This is not the only thing the professor objects to, but it will serve as an example. It is apparently a formal petition addressed to the authorities here—so it starts out. Then it says that double whiskey-and-sodas be served to each student in his bed before breakfast because the menace to student health in having to walk to the dining room on an empty stomach is appalling. And here again at the end: That double whiskey-and-sodas be served to each student in his bed before retiring because the menace to student health in having to go to bed sober is appalling. The professor wishes to say that these are very presumptuous demands."

"And this about the Scottsboro Boys," said the professor with considerable effort and even more emotion.

(We had referred to an outstanding civil rights case in America at that time.)

"Oh, yes," said the interpreter. "The professor feels very strongly about that. You have here in your petition: That the Scottsboro Boys be set free immediately."

Mark and I looked at each other; it was going to be difficult.

He began, "Our petition was not serious. In fact, nothing in the whole paper was meant to be serious."

"How could we free them here in Russia?" the professor asked. "It is important case and we talk about it much here. But we can do nothing."

"We didn't mean it that way," I said. "You know the petition that the student executive committee presented last week? Well, our petition was by way of being a parody of that."

"A parody?" said the interpreter, baffled for the first time. "What is a parody?"

"Well, if someone writes something and you write an imitation of it that's funny or exaggerated—" Mark began.

"I thought your word for that was 'satire,'" the interpreter said.

"They're not quite the same thing, A satire has a purpose. It's trying to prove or correct something, while a parody is just humor for the sake of humor."

"Humor for the sake of humor?" The professor digested the words as he repeated them. "We do not have such in the Soviet Union." And so ended our disciplinary session.

Besides lectures in varying calibers of English, the course I took featured visits to courtrooms and penal institutions in the Moscow area. We were taught, among other things, that all punishments were designed for re-education and rehabilitation; and in keeping with this principle of Soviet jurisprudence, the maximum prison sentence was ten years, even for murder. The death penalty was reserved for "crimes against the state." Thievery and prostitution, we were told, still existed as hangovers from the old regime, but they were on their way out as their practitioners learned new trades in a society free of unemployment. According to our instructors, there were no political prisoners in any of the institutions we visited, and I don't think any of us asked any questions about that phrase "crimes against the state." It was not until after the assassination of the Leningrad Party boss Sergei Kirov the following winter that the infamous "purges" became a matter of world attention.

What seemed truly revolutionary to our accepting ears was a society already practicing what only the most advanced criminologists in the West were even proposing: an emphasis on curing criminal behavior instead of just punishing it. A group of us were crossing the yard of the largest prison in Moscow when an inmate in his late thirties accosted me in very American English. He wanted to know if I was familiar with New York City. When I admitted as much, he asked me if I knew of "the Tombs," as the main jail in Manhattan was then called. I responded affirmatively, and, in answer to a follow-up inquiry, acknowledged an awareness of Sing Sing prison in Westchester County. "Well, let me tell you," he said, "I've been in the Tombs and I've been in Sing Sing, and this is the best goddamn jail I've ever been in!" His enthusiasm seemed quite genuine.

I didn't delude myself that a couple of months in the country made me an expert. I had, however, read a number of books about the Soviet Union before I went there, and it seemed reasonable to trust the ones that checked out on the points I was able to confirm firsthand. By the same logic, I could disregard authors who made statements that were contradicted by my personal experience. The best-known hostile accounts of the Soviet Union described the suffering and misery of the Russian people under the Communist regime; even during that bleak time in Moscow, however, I found far more faith and positive thinking than in Western Europe and America. So the books that presented a different picture were not to be trusted, I concluded. On the other hand, a fairly sympathetic volume by Walter Duranty, the Moscow correspondent of the *New York Times*, and a quite partisan one by Maurice Hindus seemed to bear out my observations.

An evening I spent in Moscow with Duranty himself did much to fortify this attitude. Later portrayed by *Times* colleagues and superiors as a sort of journalistic *apparatchik*, Duranty was charming and erudite, and when I told him about our wall newspaper he took a special interest in a comic political proclamation that I had written entitled "The Tory Anarchist Manifesto."

"Where did you hear about tory anarchism?" he asked. When I told him I had made up the phrase, he assured me that there was a "movement" of the same name already in existence, also conceived as a parody of standard political doctrines. He was one of the three members of the elite group, he confided. The others were Franklin Roosevelt and his ambassador to Moscow, William Bullitt.

In retrospect, my credibility test—rejecting everything negative that I found in books or articles containing anything I considered unfair— was less than rigorous, and it led me to dismiss almost any criticism of the Soviet Union, whatever the source. In the years that followed, I was troubled by the glorification of Stalin and the startling number of Bolsheviks confessing to conspiracies against the party and the state. Yet no less an authority than Joseph Davies, who succeeded Bullitt as U.S. ambassador, attended the show trials and attested to their legitimacy, and I chose to accept that woefully naïve verdict. For the next ten or fifteen years, I treated every piece of antagonistic writing about the Soviet regime with the automatic skepticism that I might have applied to an argument in favor of the Inquisition or reincarnation.

Much later on, I had to admit to myself that part of the reason I found life in Moscow so pleasant for others was the quite pleasant life I personally was living. There was one particularly attractive young woman among my fellow students and another in a group from Sarah Lawrence College with whom I had shared a train compartment from Leningrad to Moscow. My budget, which had seemed fairly austere when I embarked, turned out to be quite sufficient to cover the creature comforts that mattered most: a group of us could linger over a heaping plate of caviar and a carafe of vodka for a total cost of less than fifty cents.

On returning to America, I followed John's and Jim's examples by making an appointment with Stanley Walker, the city editor of the nation's most literate newspaper, the *New York Herald-Tribune*, where Jim was now a reporter and which John had just left to launch his own syndicated sports column. Jobs were in very short supply in those depression years, but the family name was a valuable asset, and Walker was a fan of Dad's. With an air of mystery, he spoke of a job that he would be in a position to offer in a couple of months at an unexpected location. It turned out to be the Hearst tabloid, the *Daily Mirror*, best known for the much-read, much-feared gossip column by Walter Winchell. Walker had accepted the job of managing editor there in the misguided hope of transforming the *Mirror* into his idea of a newspaper for ordinary New Yorkers. It took no more than a couple of months for him to learn that only William Randolph Hearst was allowed to have ideas on that subject. But while Walker soon resigned and went to work for the *New Yorker*, I stayed on as a reporter for almost all of the year 1935.

On a typical working day, I covered half a dozen stories in farflung parts of the city, phoning in my reports to the rewrite men, who composed the actual stories that appeared in the paper. (With two of them, Gordon Kahn and John McNulty, friendships began that would grow during their later careers in Hollywood and on the *New Yorker* respectively.) As the newest and youngest member of the city staff, I was assigned mostly to stories of lesser import: suicides, accidents, minor murders, burglaries, and (equally inconsequential in the *Mirror's* view of life) strikes. Actually, that year was an important one for the labor movement; it saw the founding of the Congress of Industrial Organizations and the first big undertaking of the New

Deal, the Works Progress Administration. My job brought me into contact with pivotal figures in the newly-aroused working class. These encounters, along with the reading of Marxist works I had begun after my trip to Russia, served to strengthen my already radical inclinations. But no amount of reading or discussion could have equaled the impact of just seeing and hearing and feeling what was going on around me in America's largest city at the lowest point in our economic history.

Writing at the height of the Clinton boom, it takes a certain effort to summon to mind the misery and desperation of those years. Unemployment, homelessness, and hunger had reached such proportions that it hardly seemed a stretch of the imagination to believe that the whole system had collapsed for good—that it was time for capitalism, with all its injustices and its cultivation of avarice, to be replaced by a more rational and equitable social order. Like most of my friends, I sympathized with many of the early New Deal reforms but didn't expect them to solve the country's deep-seated economic problems. As it turned out, I wasn't wrong. It took a world war to significantly relieve the distress of the depression.

An equally strong reason for regarding the Communist Party favorably was its unequivocal stand against fascism right up to and, some of us believed, even after the Hitler–Stalin pact of 1939. As a consequence of my observations and my reading of radical publications, especially the Communist weekly, *The New Masses*, I cast my first presidential vote, in November 1936, not for Roosevelt, Alf Landon, or even Norman Thomas but for Earl Browder on the Communist ticket. By then, I was already settled in Southern California, and it may have been that first exercise of the franchise that triggered the FBI surveillance of me that would last for decades. I had assumed, of course, that I was enjoying the vaunted American privilege of the secret ballot. On a wall outside my polling place on

Wilshire Boulevard, however, was a compilation of the district's registered voters: Democrats, a long list of names; Republicans, a somewhat lesser number; and "Declines to State," one, "Ring W. Lardner,
Jr." The day after the election, alongside those lists were posted the
results: Roosevelt, so many; Landon, so many; Browder, one.

Marx appealed not only to my sense of justice but to a taste for
rationality that my parents had helped instill in me. I had arrived at
my political allegiance, I believed at the time, purely through rigorous intellectual inquiry and analysis. Later, when I began to realize
how much I had deceived myself about what really went on in those
regions where communism was supposedly being put into practice,
and how the reality reflected on the theory, I started to wonder
whether there wasn't an emotional factor at work. In addition to those
other motivations, I came to believe, I had been fulfilling the same
old defiant impulse embedded deeply in my childhood.

The most important relationship I developed on the *Mirror* was
with Ian McLellan Hunter, a British sea captain's son who, after
coming to this country with his family as a teenager, had proceeded
directly from an American prep school to a reporter's job. Only nineteen when he first showed up (that was also my age), he then decided to enroll at Princeton, arriving there the fall after I left. His college career lasted only a year, though, and when he returned to the
paper, we began a friendship that continued and deepened until his
death in 1991. In New York, Los Angeles, Mexico, and New York
again, Ian and I were neighbors and collaborators, working on six
screenplays (the first and last about forty years apart), and during the
Hollywood blacklist, pseudonymously, on more than a hundred TV
episodes, including five pilots that became series. There was a meeting of minds between us that allowed for a harmony that we never
experienced in other writing partnerships. After six years of uninter-
rupted collaboration in the blacklist era, we continued to consult

each other on our work, and as I began to lose my brothers one by one, we spent ever more nonworking time together, playing poker and tennis and cross-checking answers on crossword puzzles and acrostics, an endeavor in which Ian excelled.

Ian, too, had an alcohol problem—one that, unlike mine, increased in severity to the point of debilitation. During the period when we had to come up with an episode for a half-hour television program every week, there were times when I had to perform the task by myself. On occasion, he would pull himself together and make a big effort to match what I had done single-handed. Eventually, though, he came to the conclusion that he would have to give up drinking for good. And he proceeded to do just that, first by enlisting in Alcoholics Anonymous as he went cold turkey, then, to fortify his abstinence, by substituting marijuana for alcohol. It happened that a friend of ours, the blacklisted writer Waldo Salt, had made the same medicinal switchover. Since Ian and Waldo also shared a love of drawing, they could pool the cost of a model and spend an evening indulging in pot and art. Neither of them drank again, as far as I know.

Some years earlier, when the film community was still disproportionately Jewish, my good friend Paul Jarrico announced a discovery. He had been wondering why a small group of his fellow screenwriters—Ian, Dalton Trumbo, Hugo Butler, Michael Wilson, and I— were such a close, cozy group. What bound us together, Paul reported, was the fact that we were all gentiles. "Nonsense," Ian declared when I passed this on to him. "It's that we're all drunks." Instantly, I knew he was right. It was by far the stronger bond.

We worked hard and drank hard. Our main form of relaxation was to gather not in a public place but in one of our Hollywood living rooms (usually Trumbo's, because he always bought or rented large houses), have a few drinks, eat a little something, and have a few more drinks. Some or all of our wives might also be on the scene, but as the liquid consumption added up, they tended to re-assemble by themselves or go home one by one, leaving behind a group and mood that became progressively more masculine.

I became fond of alcoholic beverages when I was fourteen and in my second year at Andover. The longest I have ever gone without them was my nine and a half months in Federal confinement. I've tried my hand at voluntary abstention, too, but it's never lasted more than a month or two, and from the age of forty-five to about sixty, my pattern was pretty much that of the traditional alcoholic. As of this writing, I have made it through a quarter century binge-free, steadily consuming the equivalent of one or two drinks a night.

But this is an impossibility or close to it, according to the official doctrine of Alcoholics Anonymous. AA acknowledges the existence of a species known as the "controlled drunk" who, because of fixed working hours or other obligations, only begins when his daily responsibilities have been met; and the "periodic drunk," who leads a more or less normal existence for weeks or months at a time before finding release in sustained periods of indulgence. Once an alcoholic has reached the stage where he or she has to be forcibly prevented from continuing to drink, however, the only solution—the only chance of regaining one's health, according to AA doctrine—is to go on the wagon. In the end, however many times he may fail, a drunk has to face the fact that he can never drink normally, that the one and only way out is to give it up permanently. Even ten or twenty years later, if he deludes himself into thinking he can finally handle social drinking, he will soon find himself back in the old pattern.

That is what is supposed to happen, but it didn't happen to me. I resolved to retain the pleasures of alcohol, especially its value as a sedative, without the pains of acute alcoholism. To accomplish this, I had to convert myself from an uncontrolled drunk into a controlled one. What made this improbable or even impossible according to orthodox thinking was my forty-five-year history of increasingly unrestrained indulgence.

During my first year at Princeton, the destination was a speakeasy in Trenton; by the next fall, 3.2 percent beer had been legalized, and the Nassau Tavern re-opened its bar after fifteen years to serve it. (Dad wrote a song a few months before he died: "They'll never have six percent singing on three and two-tenths per cent beer.") And then, on January 1, 1934, the whole Prohibition farce ended, and we began learning to appreciate the merits of imported, properly aged whiskey. When the working day ended at the *Daily Mirror* on East 45th Street near First Avenue, a few of us would adjourn to Tim Costello's Bar and Grill on Third Avenue and 44th, decorated with original murals by James Thurber. One or two nights a week, I would be careful to remain sober enough to make drinking money at a near-by bridge club, sometimes in partnership with my brother Jim, who was writing the bridge column for the *New York Herald-Tribune*. I couldn't have gotten by without that supplement: My salary was twenty-five dollars a week, and a first-class scotch-and-soda cost twenty-five cents.

I believe it was while working for Selznick International in Culver City that I began occasionally to have a couple of cocktails before lunch, but there were many days when I didn't drink at all because of work or, after I joined the Communist Party, political commitments. For the next couple of decades, there were short periods of abstinence plus the enforced one in prison, and, in between, intervals when I was more likely to end up drunk and a disgrace to my wife and children. Then came 1960.

There were three deaths at the beginning of that year in which I became a daily drinker: a dear friend in January, my mother in February, my brother John in March. After that, I had to get quite drunk most nights simply to go to sleep. Except for brief, abortive efforts to stop, this pattern continued until 1976. It was hell for my family, but didn't stop me from doing good work on *The Cincinnati Kid* and *M*A*S*H*, and on a book about my parents and brothers. On two occasions, desperate to lick the problem, I committed myself to strenuous detoxification programs only to find myself unable to maintain the permanent sobriety they were after. Then I tried to stop drinking on my own. On the second day of this attempt, I was having lunch with a publishing executive when I blacked out. When I came to, I found myself strapped to a bed in a hospital alcoholism unit. Again I went through the detox process and the Alcoholics Anonymous sessions until I was judged ready to continue my recovery on my own.

This time I think it lasted close to two months before my thirst reasserted itself. I decided then to try a whole new approach. Getting to sleep had been a major problem. I would lie in bed thinking about how effective strong drink had always been as a sedative; so I hit on the idea of using alcohol only at night for the double purpose of getting to sleep and satisfying my craving for the stuff. A necessary part of my program was secrecy, especially from Frances, my wife, who believed implicitly in AA's ideas, which she had first absorbed in meetings of its spinoff group, Alanon. I knew she would take my proposed experiment as just another rationalization in the service of a fatal habit.

Concealing from your wife that you are consuming eight or more ounces of booze a day requires a certain amount of covert enterprise. You have to find hiding places for your liquor—in my case, almost exclusively vodka, the drink with the least detectable smell and the incidental benefit of being available at low prices, so that the monetary expense, at least, was not a serious drain on the household. Nevertheless, on perhaps six occasions over twenty-some years, either by taking a sip for herself of what she assumed to be a soft drink, or by deliberately deciding to check up on me, Frances has found that I am still drinking. In each case I have confessed to a temporary lapse, and she has insisted that it must never happen again or she will leave me forthwith. I have made the pledge each time, and, after a brief attempt to live up to it, returned to solitary, late-night imbibing.

The situation became more complicated a few years ago, when our primary care physician, Dr. Edgar Leifer, prescribed coumadin for my atrial fibrillation, adding a stern warning about the danger of mixing this medication with alcohol. But I went on mixing them: 2.5 mg. of coumadin in the morning and half a pint of vodka in the evening. Perhaps separating the two as much as possible has had a mitigating effect; or perhaps doctors issue that kind of warning on minimal evidence, especially when they know, as Dr. Leifer has long known, that the patient has an alcohol problem; or perhaps there is a real danger, as he says, but it's a cumulative one. Even if there was a way of knowing the precise effect on my physical decline, I'm not sure I would regret my drinking. I don't think I could have finished this book (and a great many other writing projects) without it.

One of the benefits of working in the city in 1934 was the opportunity to see a lot of my brother Jim. A couple of times, our respective papers assigned us to the same story, and after he took over the bridge column on the *Herald-Tribune* and I became the bridge specialist at the *Mirror*, we often found ourselves covering the same tournament. In one case, there was a separate tournament for the newspapermen in attendance. We entered as a team, reaching the semifinals.

My social life was largely confined to two newly legitimized speakeasies, Tim Costello's and, alongside the rear entrance to the *Herald-Tribune* on West Fortieth Street, an establishment informally known as Bleeck's after its proprietor. When Prohibition was repealed, a sign appeared identifying it as the "Artist and Writers Restaurant, formerly Club." (My brother John said that Jack Bleeck knew a number of writers but only one artist. John subsequently organized a group he called the Formerly Club.)

Time spent in either establishment was devoted about eighty percent to drinking and twenty percent to eating, and all of it to man-talk at various levels of intoxication. Bleeck's, from which women had been barred during Prohibition, retained that policy for the first couple of years after repeal; and any place like Tim's that was more bar than restaurant was sure to have a much greater male than female clientele. "Respectable" women in those days would not go into such an establishment without (or sometimes even with) a male escort.

After Dad's death, Mother moved to an isolated farm in New Milford, Connecticut, and we brothers spent most of our vacations from college and days off from work there in surroundings free of the presence of young females. The result (and perhaps also the cause) of this stag social life was that the three of us lagged behind in the normal teenage drive for sexual experience and a love life. Our youngest brother David was less inhibited. Before he was three years old, he had added an imaginary sister to our ménage. Her name was Alice Heinzie Blue.

John Lardner was already known for his byline stories in the *Herald-Tribune* when, at the age of twenty-one, a matter of weeks after our father's death, he began his own nationally-syndicated sports column. Jim was not yet twenty when he, too, went to work for the *Herald-Tribune* in 1934, and he moved on to its Paris edition about three years later. I had my first national magazine piece published when I was eighteen and had finished my first Academy

Award–winning screenplay before my twenty-sixth birthday. There were indications before David's death at twenty-five that he might have turned out to be the most versatile writer of us all. At twenty, he began doing pieces for the *New Yorker's* "The Talk of the Town" section; during the next few years, he took on "Tables for Two," the nightclub column, a new feature called "Notes on Sports" and (when the magazine's movie critic died) "The Current Cinema." Because the *New Yorker* had a policy against having the same byline appear more than once an issue, his three columns were signed, respectively, "D.E.L.," "D.L." and "David Lardner."

One of his early assignments as a movie critic was *The Cross of Lorraine*, on which I was one of six official writers, three associated with the script, and three with the story. In his review, which was lukewarm on the subject of the picture's overall merits, David dealt with this morass of credits by stating that there were just too many writers involved to warrant mentioning them individually.

Of course, one reason we brothers could imagine the possibility of becoming writers and our father couldn't, was that we had his example to follow. We also had the benefit of his observations on language and the finer points of journalism. There had been no one in his immediate environment making a living as a writer, and he had originally been more interested in writing songs than prose. What changed all that was a stroke of fortune. The writer of the *Chicago Tribune's* most popular column, "In the Wake of the News," died and Dad was asked to take over. For the first time, his professional work incorporated the mixture of poetry, parody, nonsense and ungrammatical English that he had played around with in his letters. It was for the column that he wrote a series of verses that were collected into his first book, *Bib Ballads*, in 1915. Addressed to his son John, they dealt lightheartedly with the universal emotions of first-time parenthood:

One thing that's yours, my little child
Your poor old Dad is simply wild
To own. It's not a book or toy;
It's your imagination, boy.
If I possessed it, what a time
I'd have, nor need to spend a dime

I wish that I could get astride
A broom, and have a horse to ride;
Or climb into the swing, and be
A sailor on the deep blue sea.
Or b'lieve a chair a choo-choo train
Bound anywhere and back again.

Jim and David died too young for anyone to know what they might have accomplished, but I think it's safe to say that neither John's best writing achievements nor mine approached Dad's level of distinction. On the other hand, it is also true that we were more advanced in our different branches of the craft than he was at the age of, say, twenty-five.

John was the most like Dad in size and speech, devotion to sports (even as he, too, wrote about many other subjects), and the respect he drew from colleagues, especially journalists. His health, too, began to decline at about age forty due to a severe, long-neglected case of tuberculosis followed by a series of heart attacks, and, in John's case, multiple sclerosis. That diagnosis, he told me, was the final blow, making him reject an offer to become theater critic for the *New Yorker*. He was afraid his symptoms would show as he walked down the aisle.

His fatal heart attack occurred just six weeks after we had stood at Mother's bedside and jointly advised her doctor not to take

extreme measures to keep her alive as a hopeless invalid. The shock
of his death retrospectively strengthened me in our decision about
Mother. Extending her life would only have brought her the opportunity to learn that the fourth of the five men in her life was gone.

Jim had been the second, almost five years to the day after Dad.
Spain had abandoned its medieval regime for a modern democracy,
the last country in Western Europe to do so, in 1931. The elections
of 1936 brought a popular, left-leaning government to power, and the
defeated right-wing forces—led by "five insurgent generals" with
Francisco Franco at their head—launched a military revolt. Soon
Mussolini and Hitler joined the rebels, supplying troops, tanks, and
planes. In response, volunteers from around the world—including
Italian and German exiles—formed an International Brigade to
assist the undermanned, underequipped government forces.

My own ardent partisanship for the Loyalists, as the democratic
forces were known, was intensified when Jim, at twenty-four, went to
Spain to cover the war for the *Herald-Tribune*. He had been discour-
aged by some of his *Tribune* duties, which included translating,
rewriting, and waiting outside a chateau in southern France to hear
whether Wallis Simpson would be married on Wednesday or Friday.
Still, though he evidently spoke of enlisting before he left Paris at the
end of March 1938, I believe he had concluded that he could do more
for democracy in Spain as a journalist than as a soldier. He changed
his mind after covering a battle between the Internationals and Italian
Fascist regular troops, and sending a long, detailed account back to
his editors. His story wound up being cut to a couple of negligible
paragraphs in favor of a lead piece by Vincent Sheean, a best-selling
author who, ironically, had become Jim's closest friend in Spain.
To Jim's marvelously logical mind, reality had proven his earlier
assessment wrong. Against the urgings of both Sheean and Ernest
Hemingway, with whom he had shared a train compartment from

Paris to Barcelona, Jim volunteered for the Lincoln Brigade, as the American battalion was called. And when his superiors, afraid of adverse publicity if he were killed, assigned him to a behind-the-lines unit for misfits, he deserted to the front. In a letter to Mother, he cited his main reasons for volunteering:

"Because I believe that fascism is wrong and must be exterminated.

"Because my joining the I.B. might have an effect on the amendment of the neutrality act in the United States.

"Because after the war is over I shall be a more effective anti-fascist.

"Because in my ambitious quest for knowledge in all fields, I cannot afford in this age to overlook war.

"Because I think it will be good for my soul."

He was wounded in his first combat action and spent six weeks convalescing before he returned to combat duty. As a corporal in charge of a scouting patrol, he told his men to wait while he investigated some sounds on a hill ahead. His men heard a shout in Spanish and Jim's voice challenging in the same language. The enemy on the hill then replied with enough machine-gun fire and hand grenades to repel a full-scale attack. He was killed, it turned out, on the night before all the Internationals were withdrawn from the Loyalist side in the war.

"In the short time he was with us," Milton Wolff, commander of the Lincoln Battalion, said later, "and despite his extreme natural shyness, he won the friendship and respect of everyone in the battalion. He was looked up to both as a man and as a soldier and he won his rank of corporal quickly by hard work and courage.

"What he did was an unusually courageous thing—going ahead alone in no-man's land in the middle of the night and leaving his two men behind because he did not want to risk the safety of anyone but himself."

Mother, who had opposed America's entry into World War I on pacifist grounds, attributed his death to a noble delusion. For me, it was the most shattering of all the family deaths. We had always been close—so close as children that when people inquired about our whereabouts, we became a unit known as Jim-and-Bill or Bill-and-Jim. Along with the terrible loss, I felt an irrational sense of guilt that I hadn't been the one to join up instead of staying home and tasting the joys of first fatherhood. And remembering the many conversations in which we had talked domestic and global politics, I wondered how much of an influence I might have had on the thinking (not that he couldn't think for himself) that led him to such an early end.

It was hard to be a journalist in those years without feeling the urge to cover the struggle against fascism. Disqualified for military service by his eyesight, David finagled his way to London under the auspices of the Office of War Information in July 1944, and then, in September 1944, somehow managed to get the press credentials he needed to move on to France, where he began reporting for the *New Yorker*. The magazine published his first article from overseas—a "Letter from Luxemburg"—in mid-October. A few days later, David and a fellow correspondent, Russell Hill, went by jeep to Aachen, Germany, which had just been captured by the Allies. Returning with blackout lights on a dark night, the jeep drove off the road and hit a pile of mines. Hill survived; the driver was killed almost instantly; David died in a hospital without regaining consciousness. In the next issue, an obituary signed "The Editors" concluded with the words: "We liked and admired him as much as any man we have known, and we have never printed a paragraph with deeper sorrow than we print this one."

John heard the news first through the magazine they both worked for. He went to the hotel where Mother was staying while doing volunteer war work as a nurse's aid. We got a message to David's wife

Frances, a radio actress, asking her to come to their apartment as
soon as she was through with her day's work. John tracked me down
at Dalton Trumbo's house in Beverly Hills and urged me to get to
New York if I possibly could, to help out. Wartime travel was strictly limited by military priorities, but I was on a plane the next day
through the influence of James Cagney, with whom I was working on
a movie (never made, alas,) about George Armstrong Custer.

The children, Katharine and Joseph, were twenty-one months and
six months old, much too young even to be told what had happened.
Frances, who had leading roles on *Topper* and *Terry and the Pirates*,
resolved to continue with both, not just for the money but in order to
maintain a household routine. For Mother, though friends and relatives swiftly appeared from all over, the force of this third blow was
beyond fathoming. More than a month passed before she was able to
resume her nurse's aid work with terminal cancer patients. After the
war, she spent most of her time in New Milford, reading, knitting,
doing crossword puzzles and cryptograms, and tending her flower
garden. That quiet routine lasted until the early fifties, when, in one
of the unpredictable repercussions of the blacklist, my family
descended on her en masse.

four "This is Mrs. Norman Maine"

WHILE working on the *Mirror*, I kept in touch with the Swopes, and it was the well-connected Herbert Bayard Swope, Sr., now a speechwriter for Franklin Roosevelt, who greased the wheels for my entry into the movie business. At a party he gave in Sands Point in the summer of 1935, Swope introduced me to his producer-friend David Selznick, who sounded me out about working in Hollywood. Some of the most important writers in the New York newspaper world had already made the leap, and when Selznick came through with a job offer a few months later, the insignificance of my work on the tabloid made the decision an easy one for me. That November, I boarded an airplane for the first time in my life on what was supposed to be a twenty-four hour flight to Los Angeles.

Air travel was certainly not for the masses in those days. Our pro-
peller-driven biplane carried fourteen passengers, its full comple-
ment; they included the playwright John van Druten and the movie
star Miriam Hopkins. At St. Louis, the second stop, we were informed
that because of rough weather ahead we would proceed to Denver by
overnight train. About twenty-four hours later, in Denver, we were put
on another plane and flown to Los Angeles with, I believe, just one
stop on the way. Our pioneer ancestors would never have believed it.
We had crossed the continent in less than three days.

Southern California was a strange and remote territory in 1935,
and a very appealing one to a twenty-year-old who had grown up in
the Northeast. In that relatively traffic- and smog-free era, the cli-
mate and the sense of open space came as a happy shock to the system. The Depression was far less visible than it had been in New
York, and a comfortable life was well within the means of a single
man on a Hollywood payroll, even a junior publicist, as I was to
become. But the main attraction, of course, was the movie business.

Almost all the pictures being made at the time were produced,
distributed, and initially exhibited by one of six major studios within a few miles of each other in Hollywood, the San Fernando Valley,
and Culver City. Only Samuel Goldwyn had set himself apart, making one movie at a time and fussing over it. Now David Selznick, at
the age of thirty-two, was going to follow in Goldwyn's footsteps by
leaving Metro Goldwyn Mayer and launching a production company
of his own.

As a teenager, David had apprenticed with his father, Lewis, a
silent-movie mogul, before working as assistant to B. P. Schulberg,
the head of production at Paramount, and, most recently, as a producer for R.K.O. and M.G.M.

In his new venture, he would be moving a mile east to Culver City,
where his financial backer, the wealthy John Hay ("Jock") Whitney,

had leased a whole studio for him. The main building, at one end of which David settled his production staff of four women and three men, was a large, colonnaded colonial structure resembling George Washington's mansion at Mount Vernon. Its image became the company logo.

In assigning me to the publicity department, David probably had two thoughts in mind. One was to make use of my newspaper experience. The other, since my duties would require me to spend a lot of time on the set of the production of the moment, was to give me an incidental education in the basics of moviemaking. The department was quartered in a small cottage of its own. The personnel consisted of publicity director Joseph Shea, whom Selznick had recruited from Fox Films (merging that year with a new company called Twentieth Century), a secretary, and Shea's assistant—me.

David's way of making movies was far different from anything we know today. A few years ago, a critic ruminating in the *New York Times* on the ever-popular subject of who deserves to be considered the true author, or *auteur*, of a motion picture, triumphantly announced his discovery that several old pictures he had liked from the 1930s were the work of the same director, John Cromwell, among them *The Prisoner of Zenda*, starring Ronald Colman, Douglas Fairbanks, Jr., and Madeleine Carroll. Reading still further, however, the critic learned that "the front office" had been dissatisfied with two important sequences in *Zenda* and had ordered them rewritten and reshot, one by George Cukor, the other by Victor Fleming. Nevertheless, the critic continued, "The result is nothing less than a first-class miracle; the many cooks hadn't spoiled the fun, the whole tasty conceit still hangs together. It is difficult, however, to see how Mr. Cromwell could be called the work's *regisseur*, its *auteur*, its daddy."

Difficult indeed, for, as he failed to notice or omitted to mention, "the front office" on that 1937 production was David O. Selznick, and

Zenda evolved through a style of filmmaking that not only doesn't exist today but existed then only in pictures produced by Selznick himself and, to a lesser extent, by Goldwyn, Irving Thalberg, and Hal Wallis.

There certainly was an *auteur* on a Selznick picture, and it was not the director or the writer. At the age of thirty, Selznick had been given an independent production unit at M.G.M., the domain of his father-in-law Louis B. Mayer. At M.G.M. and again two and a half years later as president of the grandly named Selznick International Pictures, he perfected the method of handcrafting one movie at a time. To him, producing meant shepherding every step of the process: the choice of subject, scriptwriting, casting, designing, shooting, scoring, editing, and marketing. Not a detail in any one of these areas escaped his close attention.

When a writer had written and rewritten a scene to Selznick's specifications, David would tell him what he expected to find in the next scene, and dictate final corrections in the scene he had just okayed. Each costume, each set, each choice of location was only tentative until he approved it. The director and film editor could express a preference from among what might be dozens of takes of a single shot, but David had the ultimate say. Customarily, he would edit parts of his current picture at night, while preparing his next picture during the day. These editing sessions often went on until morning. *Zenda* was just one of a number of pictures that, as a result of some pre-dawn inspiration of David's for improving a particular scene or sequence, went back into production long after the regular shooting schedule had ended. Even after the release prints had been shipped to the warehouse and theaters, he would be approving or rewriting advertising copy. There was no field of expertise in which he considered anyone else's judgment equal to his own.

Why didn't he direct the pictures himself? When people raised that question with David, his matter-of-fact reply was that he was too busy with more important matters. He found it more efficient simply to tell the director how to shoot the movie, and then, if the results left him dissatisfied, hire another director. That's what he did with his close friend and closer collaborator George Cukor on *Gone With The Wind*. Together they had made *A Bill of Divorcement, Dinner at Eight,* and *David Copperfield,* which rank among the great achievements of the early talking-picture era. Cukor was the only director under contract to Selznick International, and he had given a year of his time to the preparation and casting of what our little band of hype artists had convinced an anxious public to regard, long before its completion, as the greatest picture of all time.

Some years after David's death, George maintained that he still had no idea why he was fired, and David always avoided any explicit statement on the subject. Rumor had it that Cukor, known as a "women's director," was not doing justice to the film's male star. His dismissal was said to have been the result of pressure from Clark Gable and his home studio, M.G.M. But there is also evidence that David himself felt some vague dissatisfaction with what he was seeing on screen—an instinctive reaction springing from a lifelong experience with film. In any case, he summoned George to his home to tell him that he was being replaced by Victor Fleming, and the two, who had been identified professionally for a decade and bore such a physical resemblance that they were sometimes mistaken for each other, never worked together again.

Fleming had a very different reputation, as a director of adventure films and a rugged man's man. Just the same, David's brand of oversight soon drove him into a hospital with nervous exhaustion, and a third director, Sam Wood, was called in to take over for four weeks. At least two more directors also filled in for brief interludes.

Seventeen writers, in all, had worked on the screenplay. Scott Fitzgerald numbered among them, along with a succession of the most experienced and highly paid craftsmen in the movie business and five prominent playwrights—Sidney Howard, Charles MacArthur, John van Druten, Edwin Justus Mayer, and John Balderston. Nevertheless, when Fleming took over, he and Selznick decided on a drastic rewrite, and David turned to his old friend and standby, Ben Hecht.

David and Ben had known each other for about fifteen years, and each recognized the talents and shortcomings of the other. Ben was stupendously bright, with the wit, verbal dexterity, and capacity for intense concentration to write superior novels, plays, and movies. He was known also for working fast—a big plus with production costs on the suspended opus running at fifty thousand dollars a day. His screenplays include *The Front Page*, *Twentieth Century*, and *Notorious*. But he also had an insatiable mercenary streak that prompted him to make deals for no obvious motive other than money. In the case of *Gone with the Wind*, time was at such a premium that Ben, according to the best of my recollection, never even bothered to read the book; nor could he afford the luxury of inspecting more than one of the many accumulated versions of the script. Ignoring the other sixteen attempts, he went back to Sidney Howard's initial draft and used its structure to work out revisions in three-way (Selznick–Fleming–Hecht) conferences, with Ben sitting down at his typewriter after each session and pounding their decisions into screenplay form. It took him two weeks.

In accepting Swope's recommendation of me, Selznick was hardly making the kind of major gamble associated with his image. Sure, he had agreed to pay my plane fare to California and, if the experiment failed, back to New York. But in case of success, he invoked a standard Hollywood practice of the day, a long-term contract with options available to the employer only. He was bound for the first three months to pay me forty dollars a week, followed, if he so chose, by three more months at the same wage; only then would the price of my services be raised to fifty dollars. In my seventh year of servitude, I would be making two hundred and fifty a week. Not very attractive terms by present-day standards, but perfectly satisfactory when contrasted with my reporter's salary of twenty-five dollars a week.

When he hired Joe Shea, David had emphasized that he was not seeking publicity for himself personally; it was the new company, Selznick International, and its product and stars that were to be sold to the American public. Joe, who took these words literally, was summarily replaced about a month after I arrived by Russell Birdwell, to whom David gave the same self-effacing instructions. The shrewder Birdwell didn't take him seriously for a moment, and we spent a large proportion of our time contriving ways to get items about David into the gossip columns and generally helping to convert him into one of Hollywood's leading celebrities. About the time I was moving out of his department, Birdwell conceived the greatest promotional stunt of his career and movie history: the vast, closely reported and entirely synthetic search, among established stars and complete unknowns alike, for the ideal actress to play Scarlett O'Hara.

But the ploy of Birdwell's that I remember most fondly, because it illustrates both the creativity and utter phoniness of the publicity craft, began in a casual conversation with Carole Lombard on the set of another Hecht-scripted picture, *Nothing Sacred*. It was income tax time back in the days, incidentally, when there was no such thing as withholding, and whatever was owed had to be paid in a lump sum. Miss Lombard, like most highly-paid people, was complaining about the burden. "No, no," Birdwell said with sudden inspiration, "You enjoy it! You're happy to pay your taxes. That's the man-bites-dog variation." Carole, who was much smarter than most of her *consoeurs* and *confreres*, readily fell in with his scheme, and soon front pages all over the country were reporting that the co-star (with Fredric March) of the latest David O. Selznick Production considered it a rare privilege and an act of pure joy to make her proper contribution to the treasury of the greatest country on earth.

I was on the set of that particular picture the day the final shot was completed, no longer as a publicity man but as a co-author of its ending. An instant party materialized to celebrate the event. While champagne corks popped and gifts were exchanged, Carole and I renewed a conversation we had been having about an idea of mine for a movie. She broke it off when two men appeared with a present she was giving to the director, William Wellman. I thought it was odd that there were two of them since the package didn't look heavy enough to require more than a single bearer. The reason for the extra man, however, soon became clear.

"Here it is, Bill, darling," Carole announced as they unwrapped the package, "what I've always wanted to see you in." In a quick and practiced movement, her aides installed the garment on the person of the recipient. It was a straitjacket.

Carole was at the height of her career, Hollywood's leading film actress measured by either salary or box-office draw. She was also the smartest and funniest female star around. And the most profane. Fred MacMurray, after his first day working with her on a movie, was asked by his girlfriend (later his wife), "How did it go?"

"I have never heard such profanity from anybody, man or woman," he replied.

"Other than that, what's she like?"

"Wonderful."

Myron Selznick, David's rich older brother, was the agent for Carole and dozens of other movie stars. Once, when he sent her a contract to sign with his agency, Carole noticed that he hadn't signed it yet himself. So she drafted a new contract, entitling her to ten percent of his income, and sent it back to Myron. He signed without reading it.

During the remaining five years of her life, my contacts with

Carole were mostly over the phone and mostly on the subject of a movie idea of mine about a woman alcoholic. Carole loved the subject and the story as much as I, but practically no one else did. Maybe the success of Billy Wilder's *The Lost Weekend* would have helped our project, but that came only three years after her fatal plane crash in 1942 on a tour selling war bonds.

One of my favorite instructors in the ways of the movie business was Val Lewton, who had been David's story editor at M.G.M. and performed the same function at the new company. Val's attitude toward his boss and all the other studio potentates he had encountered, notably Irving Thalberg and Louis B. Mayer, was a wonderful blend of servility and contempt. The former quality came from a military school education that hopelessly addicted him to the habit of addressing as "sir" any male older than or superior in status to himself. Selznick, who was about the same age as Val, was always "Sir" or "Mr. Selznick," although twenty-one-year-old Budd Schulberg, then a lowly reader in Val's department, called him David simply because Selznick had once worked for his father. Beyond mere terms of address, Val was invariably a sorry sight in the presence of his boss, cringing and scraping and apologizing, while suffering more indignities than the rest of us in the form of abruptly cancelled meetings and long waiting periods in Selznick's outer office.

After a session with Selznick, however, Val would regale Budd and me with biting accounts of life at the top, saving his most withering language for descriptions of and quotations from our common employer. Val, incidentally, went through another five years of subservience to Selznick before emerging at R.K.O. as a producer of superior low-budget horror films like *The Cat People*, *Leopard Man*, and *I Walked with a Zombie*.

Since the function of a story department is to cover all written material which might be appropriate for a particular company to translate into film, you might think that Val, Budd, and two erudite women, Jere Knight and Elizabeth Meyer, would have more than filled the needs of Selznick International which, for all the attention it generated, produced on average less than two pictures a year. But Selznick also felt the need for a story editor in New York, a bright, confident woman named Kay Brown, whom Val viewed as his enemy in a jurisdictional struggle. It was she who sent Selznick the unpublished typescript of *Gone with the Wind* with an urgent recommendation. Far too busy to read such a long book, Selznick delegated the task to three people: Val; David's personal secretary Silvia Schulman, an intelligent, attractive young woman whom I married the following year; and me. We passed around the pages of the single carbon copy available and came up with a split decision. Val found it poorly written and not worth the money it would cost to produce. I, in my debut as an appraiser of movie material, cast another no-vote, mostly because I objected on political grounds to the glorification of slave-owners and the Ku Klux Klan. But Silvia was so enthusiastic and so persistent that David agreed to read a synopsis and began to consider it seriously. Jock Whitney, chairman of the board of Selznick International, clinched the matter. He had read the book in New York and assured David that he would buy the rights himself if the company didn't.

So, against my better (or worse) judgment, the decision was made to meet the then-sizeable price—fifty thousand dollars as I remember it. I didn't have an opportunity to make an assessment of comparable significance again until thirty-five years later, when I declined an offer to write the pilot and be head writer of the television version of *M*A*S*H*. I didn't think it had much potential as a series.

During the year of my apprenticeship with Birdwell, one of my main duties was to hang out on the sets of the two pictures in production in 1936, *Little Lord Fauntleroy* and *The Garden of Allah*;

the latter, which starred Marlene Dietrich and Charles Boyer, was a rare Selznick mistake in his otherwise triumphant decade. I was supposed to pick up little items for the syndicated movie columns (which ran in almost all newspapers at the time) and for the trade papers, whose contents were almost wholly provided by studio publicity departments. Conversing with the actors and other participants in the process was considered a crucial part of the job, for we were always trying to cook up feature stories we could plant somewhere. Actually, I probably spent more hours with less to do on the soundstage (or, in the case of *Allah*, the desert location) than anyone else connected with these productions. So I had plenty of time to observe how the various craft departments functioned in cooperation to produce a movie, which was one of the reasons I had been given the job.

The director of *Allah* was Richard Boleslavsky, who had been a theatrical giant in the Moscow Art Theater before the Russian revolution along with his fellow director Konstantin Stanislavsky. Afterward he had been an eminent director and acting teacher in Warsaw, Paris, and New York before Hollywood called. His book *Acting: The First Six Lessons* was a classic of the craft. He had been signed to a contract at M.G.M. with great fanfare and then assigned in typically inappropriate Hollywood studio fashion to a series of low-budget potboilers. The only exception was *Rasputin and the Empress*, starring Ethel, John, and Lionel Barrymore, a commercial failure. Then Columbia Pictures borrowed him to do a charming and profitable comedy, *Theodora Goes Wild*, starring Irene Dunne. But its success had no effect on studio heads Mayer and Thalberg; it was back to B-pictures for poor Boley.

Allah, with its big-name stars, sent his hopes soaring. They descended back toward earth during a shooting schedule with more than its quota of mishaps and setbacks. The location itself, a desert area near Yuma at the California–Arizona border, was dispiriting; we lived there for weeks, shooting love scenes at one hundred-and-twenty degrees in the shade, if you could find shade.

This was the one Selznick International picture with a rival *auteur* to David himself. But it was not Boley, and it was certainly not the two men whose names appeared on screen because, among a succession of writers, they were judged to have contributed most to the eventual hash of a screenplay. The force moving in on both the producing and directing functions was Miss Marlene Dietrich, whose many talents, I was to find (because it encroached on my own duties), included retouching her publicity stills. Her assumed jurisdiction also extended to the script, casting, sets, costumes, and the composition of every shot in which she appeared. Her impressive arsenal of weapons for getting her way included cajolery, tantrums, blackmail, boycott, and sexual seduction. I was the third party present at an exchange between Marlene and Joseph Schildkraut, a distinguished actor and the son of an even more distinguished one, who played her obsequious servant in the picture, which seemed but a continuation of the role he had assumed with her off-camera.

"Miss Dietrich," he said in his humblest voice after the first couple of days of shooting, "do you think there's a scene somewhere in the script where I could turn more than just my profile to the camera?" After a moment or two of concentrated thought, Marlene replied that, yes indeed, she foresaw just such an opportunity in the schedule ahead.

"It's the shot at the station," she went on, "where you're following me carrying my bags. I suddenly see the man I'm trying to avoid and I turn and walk off quickly in another direction. I don't see any reason why the camera couldn't hold on you for a moment, in full face, reacting."

Marlene made herself most unpopular on that location, at least among those of us who were not invited into her bed, but I came very close to forgiving her because of a performance she put on for half a dozen of us enjoying the comparative coolness of a desert evening. It was an imitation of Greta Garbo and her restless, acutely sensitive screen presence as superb and devastating as anything of the kind I have ever witnessed.

In the end, neither Dietrich nor Selznick, from their separate command, could do anything to save the picture from the fate it deserved. Boley proved phlegmatic on that subject. The disaster he began to scent, he assured me, would make little or no difference at his home studio. "Whether it's a flop or a hit," he told me, "it will be the same thing when I go back to Metro. My next picture will be—what is that thing you keep under the bed when there is no toilet?"

"A piss pot," I suggested.

"*Murder in a Piss Pot*, that's what they'll give me, with a twelve-day shooting schedule."

During my first months in Hollywood, I reconnected with two family friends from my childhood days, Scott Fitzgerald and Dorothy Parker. I had seen Dottie, as she was known, a number of times socially before she and her husband, Alan Campbell, came to the studio to write the screenplay of *A Star Is Born*. It was a mixed blessing, therefore, when David asked Budd Schulberg and me to read the script as it emerged and see if we had any thoughts to contribute. But when he invited us to incorporate some of our suggestions into the script, we insisted that Dottie and Alan be consulted first. To our surprise and gratification, they professed to be delighted with the setup, maintaining that they were under too much pressure to get the work done in time.

Bill Wellman, who had written the story, was also going to direct the picture. He was an engaging fellow and knew his craft well, but it was a mistake to cross him, as I soon learned. We were having a conference in Selznick's office—David, Bill, Budd and I—when I ventured to criticize a scene in which a studio publicist (Lionel

Stander) treated the troubled star (Frederic March) with what struck
me as an unmotivated extra edge of hostility.

"He's drunk," Wellman said, as if that explained everything.

Someone that nasty when drunk was probably also nasty when
sober, I countered.

"*I'm* nasty when I'm drunk," Wellman said.

"That proves my point," I replied.

Our relations were noticeably cooler after that.

With the production well underway, Selznick turned his attention
to the ending, enlisting half a dozen prestigious and highly paid
writers in the search for one. Budd and I, being on salary and close
to hand, were also instructed to apply ourselves to the problem. We
came up with a brief final fadeout at Grauman's Chinese Theater in
which Janet Gaynor—the young star recovering from the suicide of
her husband—introduces herself to a throng of admirers as "Mrs.
Norman Maine." The truth is, we had rejected that bit as too corny
when we first thought of it, but after fiddling with several lame alter-
natives, we decided it was better to submit something than nothing.
To our surprise, the results were enthusiasm all around, promotions
from reader and publicity assistant to screenwriters, and the use of
our ending in the 1937, 1954, and 1976 versions of the movie.

Dottie is often remembered for the cutting things she had to say
about people she found pretentious or otherwise distasteful. But she
had warm and generous feelings for those she cared about. I benefited from the start by being associated in her mind with my father
who ranked particularly high in her esteem. (Lillian Hellman has
reported that they had an affair, which I have several reasons for
doubting. But her attachment to Dad was obviously strong. Years
later, I spent time with her during a hospitalization for alcoholic
delusions shortly before her death; one of those delusions was a ten-
dency to confuse me endearingly with Dad, who had by then been

dead for a couple of decades.) In her on-again, off-again marital and screenwriting alliance with Campbell, it was Dottie who made all the decisions. Now she wanted Budd and me to get screen credit for our contributions to *A Star Is Born*. This Selznick properly declined to do; we hadn't written enough to deserve it. He did, however, assign us over the next few months to prepare a number of stories and proposals that, as best I can recall, he never got around to reading.

Nineteen thirty-six was also the year of my screen test—a non-event, ordered by Selznick, which helped define my career possibilities and limitations. He assigned the task to Cukor, who delegated it to an assistant. The only evidence I ever received that David had reviewed the test personally was a secondhand report: It demonstrated, he said, that I was definitely slated to be a writer. I saw the test myself about a year later, when, much to my discomfort, Budd treacherously sneaked it out of the studio film vaults and presented it at a party as "a special short subject of interest to everyone here."

Early in 1937, there was another ending crisis, this time involving *Nothing Sacred*. Ben Hecht had left town after delivering the screenplay with an ending David pronounced inadequate. The picture was a madcap comedy about a tabloid newspaper hyping the story of a young woman, Hazel Flagg, doomed by a supposedly fatal illness. With shooting almost complete, the situation was so desperate that David airmailed the script to a battery of highly-paid writers in the East including George S. Kaufman, Moss Hart, and Robert E. Sherwood, simultaneously distributing copies by messenger to a selection of top screenwriters in Hollywood. Budd and I were also given the chance to compete with this mass of talent, but when Budd fell sick on the first day of our effort, I was re-assigned to collaborate with George Oppenheimer, a contract writer for M.G.M. Of all the new endings submitted, David selected the one that we had devised, and it was shot almost precisely as we had set it down.

We suggested that the film conclude with a shot of the misdiagnosed young woman (Carole Lombard) heading off on a round-the-world cruise with the newsman who has fallen in love with her (Frederic March again). They are escaping the effects of the revelation that she is actually in fine health. When a fellow passenger tells Carole she reminds her of Hazel Flagg, Carole's response is a scornful, "That phony!"

As a result of these two episodes, I found myself hailed as an ending specialist—a decidedly premature characterization. (I don't think I've had a writing project of my own since then in which I wasn't stumped for an inordinate amount of time by the ending.) Later that year, however, Budd and I reached the conclusion that we deserved more than our sixty dollars (me) and seventy-five (him) a week. The sum we had fixed upon as equitable was, I recall, a hundred and twenty-five apiece, but in a series of meetings on the subject, the man in charge of contracts, Daniel O'Shea, insisted that the struggling new company, still absorbing its losses from *The Garden of Allah*, could not afford to pay us that much. A debate on this point was interrupted by Selznick's voice on the intercom demanding to know whether Sidney Howard had agreed to write the screenplay for *Gone with the Wind*. O'Shea replied that Howard wouldn't do it for two thousand dollars a week; he was demanding three. "Then for God's sake, give it to him!" Selznick ordered and hung up.

O'Shea picked up the thread with Budd and me: "What was I saying? Oh, yes. We're offering you a hundred a week apiece, and that's as high as we can go in a shaky year. After all, how many kids your age are making that much?" And he refused to budge. We countered by saying it wasn't so much the salary that mattered to us as it was their insistence that we sign new, long-term contracts. We agreed to work for a hundred dollars apiece as long as we were free to move elsewhere if the boss continued not to read what we wrote. We had observed him long enough to know that letting us work on scattered scenes in an established script was one thing, but he would never launch one of his grand productions without the insurance of established, highly-paid people doing the writing, directing, and principal acting. To get a screenplay read, no less produced, we needed auspices more open to new talent.

And that's how it turned out. They finally accepted our counter-proposal and when, a couple of months later, I was offered a job in the B-picture department at Warner Brothers Studio, I took it. Budd left Selznick International the following year, after collaborating on a script David professed to need so urgently that he had it raced to him in Palm Springs by motorcycle courier and then, typically, didn't read.

While we were still on the payroll, however, David intervened in our personal lives in unsuccessful attempts to dissuade Budd from marrying a gentile woman and me from marrying a Jewish one. His opposition to mixed marriages seemed strange in a man who kept rejecting Ben Hecht's requests for contributions to the cause of the Jews under British control in Palestine. They were not *his* cause, he maintained, since he was a thoroughly assimilated American who just happened to come from a Jewish background.

Silvia, who had worked for him at M.G.M. before switching to the new company, had much closer contacts with Selznick than I did, and she provided me with intimate glimpses that added significantly to my developing portrait of him. She alone was present, for instance, when he burst into tears over the news of King Edward VIII's abdication in order to marry the woman he loved. David was crying, he told her, "because it'll wreck the Empire."

She also had the job of transcribing her boss's legendary dictation. A magazine profile of him some years later was titled "The Great Dictator," and more recently a book was called *Memo from David O. Selznick*. Both dealt with his lifelong habit of dictating at great length the thoughts about every aspect of his business that seemed to flow into his mind every waking minute at such a speed that it had to be emptied at regular intervals to make room for further inspiration. He had a gadget on his bedside table that was fed from a huge roll of adding-machine tape so that he could tear off as many feet of notes as he had made during the night. These he would take into the studio as a basis for the morning's dictation.

His standard secretarial staff consisted of an executive secretary, who would take dictation when she was handy, a stenographer who doubled as executive secretary when the principal one was off duty, a straight stenographer, and a file clerk who could fill in when the memo volume rose high enough to require it. Silvia served in the first two categories at various times. But it took a shorthand expert to keep up with his machine-gun-style dictating pace and Silvia had never really mastered the technique. What she did instead was take notes and type out his messages in his style but in her own words. Since almost all of his memos went out under the heading: "Dictated but not read by David O. Selznick," he never became aware of the differences between his texts and hers.

Memo writing was by no means a substitute for oral communication. David was a steady and usually a stimulating talker, and he probably spent six hours or about a third of a typical working day in conference, reviewing or changing the work of all his departments down to the minutest detail. But he seemed to feel that the written word had a more positive effect and was less subject to misunderstanding. Also, the memos gave him the opportunity to express himself fully without having to pause and listen to what he considered less relevant contributions by others.

Various movie moguls had different ways of ensuring that their opinions received the attention they merited. Darryl Zanuck would have at least one full conference on every script, with the associate producer, writer, director, and anyone else prominently involved in the project, all invited to engage in a full, free discussion of the movie-to-be. There would also be a stenographer present, and the next day every participant would receive a transcript of Mr. Zanuck's remarks at the meeting, but not a word of anyone else's.

Occasionally, David would change his mind while dictating and insert the words "Disregard the above." The memo would be transcribed and sent along anyway, on the theory, apparently, that there was value to be found in any thinking he did out loud.

There were never any set hours of work in his office, nor any moment of an employee's time that David didn't regard as his. Since he was apt to be working at ten o'clock at night or three in the morning or on a Sunday mid-afternoon, he felt free to summon anyone he needed at any hour to get involved in the task that happened to have engaged his attention. In those days before long-distance dialing, he often called Silvia at home on a Sunday morning and named, say, three people in the East he wanted to talk to. As soon as she had one party on the line, she would instruct the operator to transfer the call to David's home and let her know when the conversation was over, so that she could proceed to the next one.

It would be an overstatement to say that he showed no appreciation for this round-the-clock service. Once, after a trip to New York on which Silvia took dictation for three days on the train en route, he bought her a present at Cartier's. It was a sterling silver combination flashlight-pencil, for recording his comments in the darkness of a projection room.

five

"He'll cut you down to size"

SILVIA and I saw each other daily at the studio that first year, and after we became friends, she confessed that when Selznick first revealed his intention to hire me, she took him to be referring to my brother John. Silvia had met John while working for RKO in New York, and she assured Selznick that I was a charming and talented fellow with acting as well as writing potential. It was her endorsement, evidently, that planted the idea of a screen test in his head.

While Budd and I were doing rewrites on *A Star Is Born* and turning them in to Silvia, she and I began a love affair that led to a decision to get married. When we shared this idea with our coworkers, everyone seemed pleased—everyone except David, who felt that I had somehow been entrapped and communicated his worry to Swope, who passed it on to my mother. Soon she arrived, accompanied by Jim, ostensibly to attend the wedding but actually to size up the situation. Concluding that we knew what we were doing, they joined our other witnesses at the ceremony in February 1937: Budd; his new bride, Virginia; his father, B. P. Schulberg; and, muting whatever disapproval they may still have harbored toward "mixed marriages," David and Irene Selznick.

Irene, in addition to being Louis B. Mayer's daughter, was a powerful force for order in her husband's chaotic life, packing him off to work in the morning and calling the office periodically to remind the paid help about obligations and engagements that David, left to his own devices, might have forgotten. He also benefited from her shrewd aesthetic sense. Even by movie-mogul standards, however, David was an avid skirt-chaser, and despite his strongly-expressed convictions about the importance of marrying in the faith, he eventually joined a small caravan of studio bosses in exchanging their original Jewish wives for younger gentile ones—in his case, for the actress Jennifer Jones, to whose comparatively modest talents he dedicated the last, least distinguished fifteen years or so of his movie career. Irene, meanwhile, went on to become a successful Broadway producer, commencing with Tennesee William's *A Streetcar Named Desire*.

On the eve of my wedding, Budd gave me a bachelor party in his father's baronial mansion, where he and his wife were nominal guests. Like David's father, B. P. Schulberg had been a high-flier in the silent-picture era. Now, owing more money than he could ever conceivably repay, he felt compelled to maintain the old standard of living lest his many creditors, sensing weakness, pounce at once. The party evolved into a poker game, and the more B. P. kept losing, the higher he raised the stakes. Jim and I won over a thousand dollars between us, something of an unexpected wedding present.

Jim stayed on in Hollywood for a week after our mother went home, and we spent hours talking about the world situation, especially the Spanish Civil War. Though I was a year younger, I prided myself on having some influence over him in matters political. So in the midst of my grief over his death the following year, these—our last—conversations came back to haunt me. I couldn't rid myself of the thought that I had encouraged him in his decision to join a war that, by then, was already lost. For a long time afterward, I was plagued by a recurring nightmare in which I had murdered someone. Sometimes the identity of my victim was fuzzy; at other times, it was inescapably Jim.

For about five years, Silvia and I had a reasonably happy marriage. During that time, we produced two fine children, Peter and Ann. Silvia quit her job and collaborated on a novel about a character based on Selznick, and I became a successful screenwriter, winning my first Academy Award. The book, which Silvia wrote with a friend, Jane Shore, was called *I Lost My Girlish Laughter*. It infuriated Selznick, who suspected that her real collaborator was me. When Orson Welles announced a dramatization of the work on his radio show, the Mercury Theater of the Air, David exerted all the pressure he could mobilize—which was considerable—to get Welles to call it off. But to no avail.

Fortunately, I had moved on to Warner Brothers, where the cinematic ambitions and amenities were more modest (in contrast to the other studio commisaries, which served three meals a day, Warners offered only one), but where a young screenwriter had a reasonable chance of seeing his work on film someday. At Warners, I was introduced to Bryan Foy and the methods by which he turned out a new B-movie every two weeks, none costing more than a miniscule two hundred and fifty thousand dollars. On the floor behind his desk were stacks of screenplays representing pictures produced in past years. The most distant stack was the most recent, with the screenplay for his latest release inserted at the bottom. The nearest stack was the oldest, its top script invariably from a picture that his unit had made a number of years before. Foy would pick up that script, glance at it to refresh his memory and hand it to the writer facing him. "Here," he would say, "This one was about speedboat racing. This time, let's do it about motorcycles."

I had barely gotten started on one venture of this kind when, to my considerable relief, one of the A-picture producers on the lot made a request for my services. He wanted me to collaborate with an imported British writer who didn't understand American ways well enough to handle parts of the story he had been assigned. It turned out to be quite an interesting project, and our work was going rather well when I managed to incur the wrath of Jack Warner, the brother who actually ran the studio, through two activities he was still fuming about a decade later when he testified before the Thomas committee. My first transgression was to organize a protest against a studio visit by Vittorio Mussolini, the Italian fascist dictator's son, who had publicly boasted about the thrill of dropping bombs on Ethiopian towns. Along with a number of other writers, I left the premises and joined a picket line outside the studio gates, while Mussolini the younger was inside as an invited guest. The other complaint against me involved a campaign to raise money to buy ambulances for the elected government of Spain. John Huston and I functioned as a two-man committee, wheedling contributions out of James Cagney, Bette Davis, and Humphrey Bogart, among others. John, I must say, was a good deal more persuasive than I was. My job was mainly to goad him into doing his spiel.

I don't know whether my political endeavors had anything to do with the fact that my A-picture efforts never reached the screen, but from Jack Warner's own testimony before H.U.A.C., they explain the studio's failure to renew my contract the next year. My reputation as a union activist apparently also made me persona non grata at Metro-Goldwyn-Mayer. Shortly after I left Warner, I collaborated with an Austrian writer on a story that we sold to M.G.M. We drove a soft bargain on the story, settling for the nominal sum of $5,000 in return for the studio's agreement to give us what seemed more important—a deal to write the script, at $250 a week apiece for a minimum of six weeks. To our unhappy surprise, however, M.G.M. chose to pay us off and placed the project in other hands. William Fadiman (brother of the critic Clifton Fadiman) was the story editor at Metro, and I was later told that he had vowed not to let me in the door because of my involvement with the Screen Writers Guild and its successful effort to win a representation election over the company union called the Screen Playwrights.

The three years that followed were so shaky from a career and financial standpoint that my mother kept urging me to give up the idea of Hollywood and return to New York, where Silvia's aunt, a successful businesswoman, had a job waiting for me. Instead, I teamed up with Ian Hunter, who had miraculously surfaced as a junior writer at M.G.M.

He got his job through the good offices of Ben Hecht, who was a friend of his sister's. Nothing much happened for Ian at M.G.M., though, and before long he went to work with me on a couple of low-budget pictures about a saint of a small-town medical man played, in the movies as on radio, by the actor Jean Hersholt, (later known for the good-works Oscar bearing his name). The titles, *Meet Dr. Christian* and *The Courageous Dr. Christian*, tell you everything you need to know about our contributions to this deservedly forgotten cycle of B-movies. But at least the pictures got made—with our scripts and our names on the screen.

The producer of the Dr. Christian pictures, Bernard Vorhaus, liked our work, and after an uncomfortable spell of unemployment, he made a deal with a minor studio, Republic Pictures, and hired us to adapt a book called *False Witness* into a movie retitled *Arkansas Judge*. But the work he found for us was far from steady, and it didn't pay much. So we had to remain receptive to other offers for our services, whether joint or individual. In 1941, Ian got a job collaborating with the lyricist Johnny Mercer on a picture called *Second Chorus*, and I got the break of my life when my friend Paul Jarrico introduced me to Garson Kanin.

Gar was a prodigy—a high-school dropout from Rochester, New York, who had served a brief apprenticeship on Broadway before directing a couple of well-regarded comedies at RKO. He and Paul had just worked together as director and writer of the Ginger Rogers comedy *Tom, Dick and Harry*. Now Gar had an idea for Katharine Hepburn: a movie in which she would play a newspaper columnist loosely based on Dorothy Thompson, who was virtually the only female permitted to express her views in print on important political and world affairs in those days. Gar had decided that he needed a writer conversant with the New York newspaper world to work on the script, and Paul had volunteered me. To further complicate matters, Gar had just been drafted into the Army, so we talked out a story line in the couple of days before he went off to training camp, leaving his share of the project to his brother Mike.

Our collaboration went splendidly. After we had fleshed out the story, Mike and I set it down in the form of an eighty-page novella, entitled "The Thing About Women." One of the big difficulties of selling a movie idea, I had decided, was getting people to read it. Most screenplays didn't read well, and the same was true of "treatments," the present-tense, outline-like format in which movie proposals were commonly submitted to the studios. To get around this obstacle, Mike and I dressed up our tale as a piece of fiction that just happened to be ready-made for the movies. It was told in the past tense by the sportswriter as he reacted to the intellectual snobbery, physical charms, and bewildering contradictions of a woman operating with serene assurance in a male-dominated world. We sent our story to Kate in Connecticut, and when she responded with enthusiasm, we knew we were in.

A year or two earlier, her backing would not have meant so much. Hepburn had made a number of movies at R.K.O., most of them of superior quality but unsuccessful at the box office. The National Organization of Motion Picture Exhibitors had gone as far as to name her in a diatribe against stars whose movies consistently lost money. (Garbo and Dietrich were also cited.) The theater owners denounced the studios for continuing to employ these proven audience-alienators, and R.K.O. responded by letting Hepburn's contract lapse.

Her response to this setback was to go back east and announce her unavailability for any movie part except that of Scarlett O'Hara in the impending *Gone with the Wind*. She was also on the lookout, though, for the right starring role on the stage, and she found it in Philip Barry's *The Philadelphia Story*. In a bidding war for the play, M.G.M. won, and with Cary Grant and James Stewart as her co-stars and George Cukor directing, the movie made Kate a box-office star once and for all.

From a Hollywood outcast, in fact, she had become powerful enough to insist that she, not the studio, pick her next vehicle. Having selected our story, Kate flew to California and, dispensing with the services of an agent either for herself or the script, took it to M.G.M. personally. She was also good enough to conspire with Mike and me to remove our names from the story before she handed it to Louis B. Mayer. This was a hedge, in the first place, against the possibility of further union-related animus against me; but it was also, in the second place, a ploy intended to extract more money from the studio than it would normally be expected to pay for the work of two unknowns. Mayer was accordingly encouraged to believe that he was reading the work of a prominent writer or writers who had chosen at that stage to remain anonymous; and, on that assumption, he agreed to Hepburn's price: one hundred thousand for her, the same amount for the story and still-unwritten screenplay, ten thousand for her agent, and a thousand for her round trip from Connecticut—$211,000 in all. There would be no bargaining, Kate decreed, and there was none. The money the studio reluctantly paid us when our names were revealed was the largest sum yet bestowed on the authors of an original screenplay. (Relieved of the obligation to pay an agents' commission, we spent some of our bounty on a new Ford—a gift to Kate as a replacement for the beat-up convertible passed on to her by her ex-lover, the wealthy aviator Howard Hughes.)

M.G.M. was the most prestigious and star-studded of the studios as well as the biggest, and the barrel-chested Mayer, who had left Russia with his parents at the age of three and grown up in poverty, was the most powerful man in Hollywood and the world's best-paid employee, having broken the million-dollar-a-year barrier in the depths of the Depression. Somewhere deep inside the man there must have been a cool, calculating business executive, but the emotional creature that you met in person was too real to be entirely an act. Mayer could break into tears or violent rages, sink to his knees to beg a favor or rush from behind his desk to knock to the floor with one punch a highly-paid actor who had described his own mother as a whore. His patriotism and his exaltation of womankind were equally extreme. Billy Wilder once saw him grab Mickey Rooney by the lapel and rebuke him loudly for conduct unbecoming the character he played in a long-running and hugely popular series of pictures about small-town America: "You're Andy Hardy! You're the United States! You're the Stars and Stripes! Behave yourself! You're a symbol!"

But Kate's influence with him at this juncture seemed almost limitless. Having convinced him to pay her price, she proceeded to reject all of M.G.M.'s contract directors in favor of George Stevens, who had directed her in *Alice Adams*. She also took charge of the search for a co-star, choosing Spencer Tracy, whom she had never met. At first, he seemed unattainable, for he had just started shooting a movie version of the book *The Yearling*. By a stroke of luck, however, the studio brass didn't like the rushes coming in from the location in Florida; so they suspended production, later to begin anew with a different script, director, and star, Gregory Peck. That left M.G.M. with Tracy on salary and no immediate use for him.

Kate and Spencer met for the first time in the office of the producer, Joe Mankiewicz. "Mr. Tracy. I think you're too short for me," she commented.

"Don't worry," Mankiewicz said with a laugh. "He'll cut you down to size."

She was thirty-four and he was forty-one. For a number of years, Kate had been in love with John Ford, regarded by many as America's preeminent movie director. Ford was Catholic and had a wife. When it became clear to Kate that he was not about to get a divorce, she began a highly publicized affair with Howard Hughes, who proposed marriage and dedicated his record-breaking flight around the world to her. Kate was tempted by his proposal until a visit to the Hepburn family home made their incompatibility apparent to both of them. Ford's reaction to losing her through his indecisiveness was to make, in swift succession, a body of work that included *Stagecoach, Young Mr. Lincoln, Drums Along the Mohawk, The Grapes of Wrath, The Long Voyage Home, Tobacco Road*, and *How Green Was My Valley*.

What Kate didn't seem to need at this point in her life was another relationship with a married Catholic and father of two children. But her career, in jeopardy a couple of years before, was rebounding; co-starring with Tracy could only help since he was one of a small group of Hollywood superstars whose every picture was a major event. By mutual consent, his name would always precede hers in the billing.

Mike Kanin and I were frequent visitors to the set, and what we saw happening there was the final blessing on the venture. When you write a love story, you hope that the actors will make it seem convincing, but you scarcely expect them to actually fall for each other. A familiar sight on a movie set comes when the director calls "Cut!" and the two lovers withdraw abruptly from a tight embrace, briskly heading off in separate directions as if to emphasize the nothing-personal aspect of their physical contact. Kate and Spence wanted to be together off camera as well as on. They lasted as a team for the rest of his life. Like Ford, he stuck to his Catholic marriage, but in name only.

For all the honors bestowed on it, *Woman of the Year* suffered a depressing switch late in the game. Shooting was over. Mike and I had left for New York on vacation, after attending a successful preview before an appreciative audience. We had been lucky, we felt, to get one of the best directors in the business, and Stevens had contributed a number of touches that helped define our characters and intensify the conflict and the comedy. He had not, however, had anything to do with casting the leads, defining the theme of the story, or choosing the location or content of any scene, and if a line or a piece of business didn't work, either Mike or I had been available to alter it. But the industry was even then beginning, in a very tentative way, to embrace the myth of the all-powerful, all-important director. Posters described our movie as "A George Stevens Production," in letters precisely fourteen times as large as the all but invisible line, "An original screenplay by Ring Lardner, Jr. and Michael Kanin." Still, the advertising copy was of no great concern to us.

What happened next was. In our absence, the studio decided to change the ending. Mayer, Mankiewicz, and Stevens all professed to have detected, in the reaction of the preview audience, a desire to see the Hepburn character get her comeuppance for trying to be an equal in a male-dominated world. We suspected that it was Mayer, Mankiewicz, and Stevens who felt this urge most deeply. Mayer, in particular, was renowned for his old-fashioned thinking about such matters. The mothers in M.G.M. movies "never had a thought in their heads except their children," Mary Astor complained after playing a few of them. Both Mankiewicz and Stevens were, we felt, fairly unreconstructed male chauvinists. But, in any case, the decision was made, and with the two writers conveniently absent, the studio engaged one of the most reactionary screenwriters in Hollywood, John Lee Mahin, who was incidentally the former president of the company union that had lost out to the Screen Writers Guild. (He was also, I have to say, a pretty good writer.) Mahin dutifully composed a scene in which a repentant Kate struggles to prepare breakfast for Tracy, and, reduced to tears by her incompetence in the kitchen, lets him dictate the balance of power in their marriage-to-come. Mike and I were permitted to rewrite some of the worst lines in this travesty before it was shot, but we weren't allowed to tamper with the basic transformation.

I can't say to what extent Kate shared our feelings. Given her place in the M.G.M. pantheon at the time, she probably could have found a way to resist. On the other hand, thinking about women's rights was much less advanced sixty years ago, and she may have been persuaded that the new ending would receive wider audience acceptance. If that was the case, she later regretted it. In the mid-1990s, while working on her autobiography, she called me. We had been out of touch for years. Nevertheless, her opening words were a brisk "Ring? Kate Hepburn. What was the original ending of *Woman of the Year*?" I recalled that it took place at ringside during a world heavyweight boxing championship, with her character attempting to fill in for Tracy, who had gone off on a bat. She remembered it fondly.

Like many other flawed scenes in which they acted together, though, it played better than it deserved to, and the reaction to the movie as a whole—the first, I believe, ever to enjoy a three-week run at Radio City Music Hall—sent Mike and me vaulting into the top ranks of our profession. The Academy Award we won in 1942 for best original screenplay only confirmed our status. Signed to new M.G.M. contracts, we wrote two scripts together before going our separate ways.

The first of these projects was an adaptation of an interesting book called *Marriage Is a Private Affair*. Our immediate supervisor had formerly been in charge of all production at another studio. He expressed warm approval of our script and made a few suggestions so minor that we happily incorporated them. Then he submitted our work to his supervisor and reported back to us that he had rarely met with such an enthusiastic reception from so eminent a source. Persuaded by this overwhelming evidence of our talent, the studio now wished to sign us to a long-term contract at substantially higher pay. As for the particular project on which we had been working, however, there had been a small hitch: Purely on the basis of the title and a synopsis that had been prepared for him, Louis B. Mayer had abruptly decided that the book was ideal for Lana Turner. Did that mean, we wanted to know, that he had not bothered to read our screenplay? "Why should he waste the time?" our producer responded. Since the subtleties in our script were beyond the capacities of that particular actress, there had to be a whole new approach to the material—a general process of, to use the producer's precise word, "cheapening" it. Whether we wanted to perform this essential function ourselves or move on to more respectable efforts, he left entirely up to us. We chose the latter alternative, and Ms. Turner did indeed appear in a movie that retained the title but little else of the book or our screenplay.

Our second effort was a rewrite job that eventually emerged as a movie called *The Cross of Lorraine* about the underground in Nazi-occupied France. We considered it an acceptable attempt to deal with current history for American audiences, but were appalled to learn that it was sent over to France after the liberation to be seen by people who had actually lived through what we had only speculated about.

Besides marriage, children, and career, my principal activities in the years before the United States entered World War II involved left-wing politics, mostly of the Communist Party kind. By the time Budd and I began working together on *A Star Is Born*, he had already joined the Party's recently-organized Hollywood branch. After I wrote a letter to *Time* magazine, using Selznick International stationery to express a Stalinist view of the Stalin–Trotsky conflict, Budd was reproached for not having reported so likely a candidate and instructed to recruit me—a task that took all of five minutes. I thus became one of about two dozen party members in Hollywood. (Five years later, the count was well over two hundred.) About half of us were screenwriters, the rest actors, directors, script readers, and office workers.

Being a communist was time-consuming. I attended events of one sort or another four or five nights a week. There were separate organizational and educational gatherings of my branch, and "fraction" meetings of Communists and close sympathizers within the Screen Writers Guild. Meanwhile, as a representative of the younger writers, I had been elected to the guild's executive board, which had all-too-frequent meetings of its own. In addition, there were the various Guild committees and similar groups like the Hollywood Anti-Nazi League, the Motion Picture Artists Committee for Spanish Democracy and, during the war years, the Hollywood Writers Mobilization and Russian War Relief. Silvia practically had to join the party so that we could see each other. Luckily, without any organized study, she had reached some pretty negative conclusions about the capitalist system and the inequities of American life. She was not a difficult convert.

Communists, like everybody else in the prewar years, had a lot to say about what was happening in Europe. But the subject matter of our official get-togethers was mostly local, centering on the organizational mechanics of the three "talent guilds"—writers, actors and directors—and our attempts to unionize such co-workers as readers, publicists, and secretaries. While there was room for a certain amount of playful banter ("If the comrade means me by that Bolshevist criticism, I'll ask him to step outside"), our discussions tended to be boring and repetitious. It might have been interesting to be part of a foreign-financed conspiracy to undermine American institutions and steal precious American secrets for the Russians, but we never seemed to get around to anything like that.

As for the Soviet Union, while we viewed it sympathetically as an experiment, no one I knew wanted to see the same formula applied in our own country—not the dictatorship, or the repression of dissidents, or the phony elections, or the subordination of the arts to propaganda. America, we were convinced, would become socialist with all its freedoms intact, which Russia had never had. With such a vision, the Hollywood party grew until we qualified to become what was known as a "section." That called for a membership meeting to elect a governing body (a section committee) with a full-time functionary (the section organizer) and to divide the members into a new set of branches, each with its own organizer, educational director, and secretary-treasurer.

Where to hold such a meeting was a problem, for it was assumed even then that to be publicly identified as a party member could mean the end of one's career in the movie business. Fortunately, a screenwriter named Martin Berkeley, who specialized in animal films (I have always maintained that he couldn't write human dialogue), stepped into the breach. Berkeley's house, which he offered to the party, was located in a sparsely settled canyon and yet equipped with a large living room and ample parking space. Our host either kept notes or had an outstanding memory. When he turned out to be an informer and testified fifteen years later before H.U.A.C., he named a record total of one hundred sixty-one people as either having been present that day or having joined the party afterward. His list was accurate on the whole, but in naming those at the meeting, he added Dashiell Hammett and Lillian Hellman, who were not there. I was and knew them well. They were clearly sympathetic to the Soviet Union and the Party, but whether they joined or not, I never knew.

That was because the Hollywood section had a special policy for celebrities. We always faced the likelihood that there was at least one informer in our midst, and what greater triumph could an informer experience than turning over a famous name or two? So the few of them who were recruited met separately in a small group with a couple of our most steadfast section leaders. Dorothy Parker and Alan Campbell had joined, I knew, because Budd had recruited them and I had been privy to the process. But I never saw either of them at what was strictly a party gathering.

With the intensification of the Spanish Civil War and the consolidation of Nazi power in Germany, the Party in Hollywood gained in numbers and influence. Relations between Party members and those who called themselves liberals or progressives were harmonious for the simple reason that we took the same positions on the major issues of the day. Our arguments, mostly friendly in those years, were over minor points. One cause on which there was general agreement was the rebellion against the legally elected government in Spain. During the final year of that conflict, I grew emotionally even closer to the anti-fascist cause as a result of my brother Jim's part in it. In Hollywood as in the rest of the country, the left-liberal amity lasted

up until August 1939, when the Nazi–Soviet Non-Aggression Pact
and the outbreak of World War II split the coalition down the middle.
From that moment until Hitler's invasion of the Soviet Union two
years later, to remain a Communist you had to believe the following:

1. That in the Munich Pact of 1938, the ruling forces of Britain
   and France had sold out Czechoslovakia and abandoned the
   policy of collective security with the purpose of turning
   Hitler against their real enemy, the Soviet Union.
2. That to forestall this plot, the Soviets had had no choice but
   to make a purely tactical deal with Germany, enabling them
   to strengthen their borders and build up their military power.
3. That their occupation of eastern Poland and southeastern
   Finland were not aggrandizing acts but necessary defensive
   moves against Germany.
4. That the best interests of the United States lay in neutrality.

I had subscribed to and articulated all these positions; and my liberal friends had listened respectfully, as had I to their counter-argu-
ments. Now, however, the question was whether to support or oppose
the war, and the debate was not so amicable. More people left the
Party than joined it during these embattled years, yet the new recruits
included my friend Dalton Trumbo, author of the stirring antiwar
novel *Johnny Got His Gun.* Trumbo had resisted my previous recruit-
ment efforts because of his strong pacifist sentiments; it was the
Party's antiwar stand that won him over. Subsequently, the events of
1941—the German invasion of the USSR and the attack on Pearl
Harbor—were so flagrant he found his pacifism no longer tenable.

Trumbo, as almost everyone called him, was a tremendously
appealing character, and I regarded it as a privilege to be his friend.
Brought up in Grand Junction, Colorado, he had moved with his wid-

owed mother to Los Angeles in the early years of the Depression. He worked in a bakery for a time, became a journalist, and published a novel (*Eclipse*) before breaking into the movie business as a reader and writer, at sixty dollars a week. Like Ben Hecht, he was renowned for his speed and had turned to the movies (and away from what he considered his more serious work as a novelist) in part to satisfy a large appetite for money; like Hecht too, he wrote some fine pictures, including *Thirty Seconds Over Tokyo* (a war movie singularly free of the heroics and hokum that sometimes characterized the genre) and *Our Vines Have Tender Grapes*, a story of farm life that, in its low-keyed simplicity, represented the direction in which many of us hoped see to Hollywood go after the war. By 1946, Trumbo's salary was three thousand dollars a week or seventy-five thousand a script, whichever he chose. Either way, he spent every bit of it, largely on improvements and additions to a dilapidated house he had purchased in the remote and inaccessible wilds of Ventura County. When the blacklist hit, Trumbo was forced to sell the place, and he had to do masses of undercover work at vastly lower prices just to get by. When he returned to the top rank of Hollywood writers in the 1960s, he also returned to his grandiose spending habits.

The party, the Screen Writers Guild, and the various Hollywood organizations devoted to the fight against fascism became the anchors of our social life in the prewar years; and when the guild won its battle against the Screen Playwrights, some of us served as missionaries or consultants to other categories of movie workers. I was assigned, for example, to advise a group at Warner Brothers who were trying to form a readers' guild. That was how I met Alice Goldberg, the extremely bright and attractive daughter of a Russian-born photographer—and how she met Ian Hunter. He was still boarding with Silvia and me, having moved with us from an apartment on Vista Del Mar to a house on Franklin Avenue, formerly occupied by Bette Davis. The readers held a meeting there, and later we had Alice over for dinner. After that, her evening visits seemed to continue without further action on Sylvia's or my part, and soon we became used to having her under our roof in the morning as well. By a happy coincidence, Ian and Alice began to make plans for cohabitation and matrimony around the time of the birth of our son Peter. When Ian moved out, his room became Peter's nursery.

By introducing Ian to Alice, I not only helped him land a wife but laid the groundwork for his entry into the Communist Party, of which she was already a member. I played a more direct role in recruiting Trumbo and his friend Hugo Butler, and the four of us and our wives gradually became fast friends who took each other's hospitality for granted. When Ian and Alice acquired a home and some professional security, we learned that they were both exceptional cooks who seemed to think nothing of having a dozen of us over for something like suckling pig or roast beef and Yorkshire pudding.

Politics drew me closer to some friends, and away from others. In 1940, Budd Schulberg gave me the manuscript of his Hollywood novel, *What Makes Sammy Run?* He was worried that its harsh treatment of a Jewish producer on the make might be construed as anti-Semitic. I was one of three readers—Maurice Rapf and Scott Fitzgerald were the others—who reassured him on this score. But later on, Budd accepted an invitation to discuss the matter with two of the more notable ideologues in the Hollywood branch of the party, John Howard Lawson and V.J. Jerome, from whom he got a harsher reaction. When the novel was published the following year, the *Daily Worker* ran a favorable review and then, a few weeks later, a critical one by the same author, who had evidently been chastised by party functionaries. The second time around, he found a number of serious faults with the book, including its failure to adequately acknowledge the party's role in building the Screen Writers Guild.

Heavy-handed criticism of this sort was fairly common in the party, and some people ignored it without suffering any harm. For Budd, however, the experience was apparently an epiphany, inspiring feelings of kinship with the Russian writers and artists persecuted under Stalin and leading him away from the movement into which he had recruited me just a few years earlier. A decade later, he testified before H.U.A.C. and, not content to clarify his own polical thinking, heaped praise on the committee and named names, which had become the inevitable, unavoidable bottom line of all such attempts to establish one's patriotic bona fides.

The German invasion of the Soviet Union put us Reds back in tune with the liberals. Mike and I were finishing the screenplay of *Woman of the Year* at the time, and the news had a salutary effect on my relations with Kate Hepburn. She was an able and dedicated proponent of the anti-Nazi cause, and our script conferences had often been preceded by arguments (respectful, in our case) about the latest developments in the war. On the day of the news that Germany had launched a massive attack on Soviet positions, we were pleased to discover that we suddenly saw the world the same way.

When Japan bombed our fleet and Germany declared war on America, the unity of purpose between Communists and liberals in the movie business solidified further. Together we forged the Hollywood Writers Mobilization, which put writers of war-related movies in touch with units of the armed forces or the administration in Washington, and coordinated the activities of writers volunteering to produce war propaganda. By then, the only obvious difference between us and the noncommunists was that we tended to devote more time and effort to the same causes.

With a wife and two children to support, I was in no danger of being drafted, but anxious to play a part in the war. So I was pleased to be invited to join the newly-formed Office of Strategic Services

(O.S.S.), the precursor of the Central Intelligence Agency, and to recommend other writers for its visual presentation unit. One of my nominees, Ian Hunter, was accepted. Just before our departure a telegram instructed me to await further word, while he was to come ahead. As it happened, a security check with the Federal Bureau of Investigation under the deranged leadership of J. Edgar Hoover, had found me listed as a "premature anti-Fascist"—the first time I or anyone I knew had heard of the term.

At what point, in Mr. Hoover's view, was anti-fascism not premature? Probably only at the moment we were at war. If the words were simply code for "communist," what harm could a communist screenwriter do to a wartime program that included selling the American people on the virtues of our Russian ally? This was, after all, the period in which the Roosevelt administration persuaded Warners and M.G.M., two studios previously noted for the Red-baiting behavior of their bosses, to produce *Mission to Moscow* and *Song of Russia* respectively, in order to establish that Russians were human beings. It has only become clear in recent years that FDR, for all his strengths, was simply afraid to challenge the entrenched power of the fanatical Hoover.

In the following months, I was approached by someone in the Marine Corps to join a film unit in the Pacific and then a telegram from the Office of War Information asked how quickly I could join director William Wyler in Moscow to work on a movie about the war effort there. In both cases, the invitations were rescinded after security checks. Finally, early in 1943, still anxious to find a wartime role, I enlisted for a trial term of ninety days in the training film program of the Army Signal Corps. This time there was no rejection.

After a brief indoctrination session in Queens (where the Signal Corps had taken over one of the old Astoria studios), I was sent to Camp Hood in Texas to write a film about America's new secret weapon, the tank destroyer. This large mobile gun was supposed to move so quickly and with such agility that it would decimate the tanks in Hitler's vaunted panzer divisions. It was good movie material and what we shot had more visual interest than most training films. Unfortunately, just as the film was ready to be shown, tank destroyers were employed for the first time in combat in North Africa, and failed so miserably that both the weapon and the film had to be suppressed.

Next, I was sent to the Cooks and Bakers School at Camp Lee, Virginia to write a short film called *Emergency Rations in the Combat Zone*. I was engaged in a debate with a couple of officers about the best visual way to present an unappealing item called a C-Ration when my wife phoned me from California to report that I was co-winner of an Academy Oscar for *Woman of the Year*. (In those days there wasn't even national radio coverage of the event.) Amid the congratulations that followed, my point about how to depict the C-ration was conceded.

Just as my trial term with the Signal Corps was expiring, I received an offer to work with Otto Preminger at Twentieth-Century Fox on a movie based upon the published diary of former American Ambassador to Germany, William E. Dodd, and his daughter Martha's book *Through Embassy Eyes*. To dramatize the rise of the Nazi Party and the Reichstag fire trial seemed to me potentially a far more significant contribution to the Allied cause than any training film I could possibly do, so I took the job on the spot.

I got along famously with Otto, a native of Austria whom old-time movie fans will remember as the prison camp commandant in Billy Wilder's prisoner-of-war movie *Stalag 17*. Otto's knowledge of matters Germanic enabled him to contribute a good deal to my research, which went speedily. What eventually threw the project behind schedule was his practice of shooting one movie while preparing another. Inevitably, problems with the current project took precedence over the future one, and he would draft the writer of the latter to help him out with the former—in this case, that early film noir

Laura. His problem was that Clifton Webb disliked most of the dialogue his gossip-columnist character had been given. Otto persuaded me to redo a line here another line there, and finally to rewrite Webb's entire part, all while receiving a salary for the Dodd story. I would run into this sort of thing with Otto again.

By the time I returned to and completed the screenplay about Nazism, it already had one count against it. Fox had just completed a costly film biography of Woodrow Wilson. Darryl Zanuck, who ran the studio at the time (and for many years to come), praised the movie to the skies after a screening; to underscore the extent of his admiration, in fact, he let it be known that if *Wilson* didn't show a profit, he would never again make a movie about history or public affairs. *Wilson* was a box-office disaster and Zanuck stuck to his word. He went out of his way, however, to express his satisfaction with my script, circulating it among his producers as a model of superior screenwriting and even offering me a contract with a raise in salary, which I declined.

Instead, I accepted an offer to do a film version of the play *Tomorrow the World* by my friends James Gow and Arnaud d'Usseau. It wasn't a particularly challenging job, since I was able to use whole segments of the original with only minor embellishments, but I felt that any way of helping spread a message about the horrors of Nazism was a wartime contribution. The play was about a twelve-year-old boy raised in the Nazi youth corps and then re-educated in democratic principles by an American uncle, portrayed in the movie by Fredric March.

My next assignment was equally on the nose. In 1945, which was also the year Silvia and I were divorced, and I was rejected by the armed services for an asthmatic condition that vanished almost immediately afterward, I was asked by the legendary but all too real studio head Samuel Goldwyn to read a novel called *Earth and High Heaven* by Gwethalyn Graham. It was a love story, set in Montreal, about the effects of anti-Semitism on an upper-class young gentile woman and an upwardly mobile young Jew. Goldwyn had bought the property at the instigation of his non-Jewish wife, Frances. Her husband was, to say the least, ambivalent: while he wanted credit for making the first American movie on anti-Semitism, he belonged to the old guard of film moguls who were so sensitive about being Jewish that they scarcely allowed Jews or Jewishness to exist in their movies. Mike Kanin and I had run into this attitude during the making of *Woman of the Year*. We had written a scene in which the Hepburn character displayed her talents as a linguist: At a party with many foreign diplomats present, she was to speak to several different guests in their own languages, among them Yiddish. That's what it said in the script. But Louis B. Mayer ruled from on high that Kate could speak Chinese, Arabic, anything we chose *except* Yiddish, and no amount of argument from anyone concerned could shake him from that edict. To the best of our ability to read his thoughts, Mayer apparently feared that an industry with a high percentage of Jews in its leadership might be accused of trying to make their culture acceptable by associating it with a glamorous star.

So it was a big step for Goldwyn to consider such a movie, even if he made a point—a repeated point—of telling me to emphasize the entertainment values of the story and avoid any suggestion of "propaganda." Bearing those words in mind, I wrote a detailed outline, and he approved it before departing on a wartime mission to the Soviet Union—a trip connected, I believe, with the movie *North Star*, which Lillian Hellman had written for him. By the time he returned, I had a first draft screenplay ready to submit. Given my own sense of him, fortified by advice from old Goldwyn hands, I had made every effort to keep the tone of the scenes as light as possible and to avoid anything that looked or sounded faintly like a pro-tolerance message. But the raison d'être of the story was prejudice—there was no escaping that fact. There was no plot development that did not spring from it. It was the theme of the novel that Mr. Goldwyn had bought and was paying me to adapt.

When I was summoned to his office to discuss the script, his opening words were, to say the least, discouraging. "Lardner," he began with an accusatory look, "you have defrauded and betrayed me." Defrauded, he proceeded to explain, because my screenplay was not what I had promised in the treatment. The few examples he cited were enough for me to see the hopelessness of the situation. The impossible dream in his head was a story in which some people were badly treated but not by anybody in particular, and others spoke out against intolerance without offending anyone who believed in it. After demonstrating to my own satisfaction, if not his, that the screenplay followed the treatment closely enough so that the charge of fraud was absurd, I asked him about the second part of his accusation. How had I betrayed him?

In an aggrieved tone he replied that one of the reasons he had hired me for the job—just one of the reasons—was the fact that I was a gentile. "You have betrayed me," he said grandly, "by writing like a Jew."

("How did you do the script?" my friend Gordon Kahn asked later. "From the righthand to the lefthand side of the page?")

In the wake of this apparently definitive conference, I began to assemble my personal belongings and prepare to leave the studio for good. I was interrupted by a knock on my door. It was Frances Goldwyn, who explained, with great trepidation, that she had never before visited a writer's office or in any way sought to interfere in Sam's business. She wanted me to know, however, how important this picture was to her. Sam, she assured me, was so knotted up inside about it that he shouldn't be held responsible for anything he might have said to me. By the time she left, I had agreed to continue working on the screenplay and, even more remarkably, to waive my salary voluntarily until I had persuaded Mr. Goldwyn that I could give him the kind of movie we all wanted but he was so nervous about.

It took another two weeks and several more highly-charged conversations with Goldwyn to make me concede that the goal would never be realized and abandon the project once and for all. At intervals over the next couple of years, however, I would see trade paper items about Goldwyn hiring yet another writer for *Earth and High Heaven*. I think there were seven in all, none of whom came up with an adaptation that satisfied him. His story editor told me that when Daryl Zanuck released *Gentlemen's Agreement,* in which Gregory Peck pretends to be Jewish in order to write an exposé of anti-Semitism, Goldwyn was indignant. Zanuck, he complained, had stolen his idea.

Later that year, a new film company teamed me up with my brother John, who had spent the war as a correspondent in Europe and the Pacific, to write a movie about Willie and Joe, the G.I.s in cartoonist Bill Mauldin's book *Up Front.* By the time we finished our first draft, the war was over and the producers backed off, claiming that no one could be sure what kind of movies would be popular in the postwar world. (A few years later, another company made a very different sort of movie from the same book.)

Tomorrow the World was released in the final summer of the war. Given the passions of the moment, its basic idea turned out to be controversial indeed. The Hollywood Writers Mobilization held a premiere for the movie and a "town meeting" to discuss it. In the film, as in the play, a Nazi-trained boy is reeducated to embrace American democratic principles. There is nothing inherently evil, the story makes clear, in the German or Japanese people—no biological predisposition to be racists or warmongers.

This may sound like an unobjectionable premise. But a great many people at that meeting did object, heatedly. Ruth McKenney, author of *My Sister Eileen* and well known for her leftist views, declared that the German people should be treated according to the principle of "an eye for an eye." The boy in the movie, she insisted, was beyond redemption: "His soul has been poisoned forever," she said. Her comments received a good deal of applause in a predominantly liberal audience. Clearly, America was not going to have an easy time getting over its own wartime hate propaganda.

The reason I had agreed to work on the movie was that I considered all theories about races or nations being superior or inferior, vicious and dangerous. When my turn to speak came, I recalled how all the countries now regarded as among the more civilized had, on certain past occasions, acted barbarously toward peoples they viewed as unworthy of respect: the British in East Africa and India, the Spanish in Latin America, the French in Indochina, the Belgians in the Congo, the Americans toward their so-called Indians and their African captives.

I did one more war movie called *Cloak and Dagger* about a nuclear physicist who goes undercover for the O.S.S. in Italy to check up on the Nazi atomic-weapons program. The star, Gary Cooper, had an admirably detached perspective on his abilities. "Keep my dialogue simple," he entreated me. "If I have to say any technical scientific stuff, nobody's going to believe I'm real."

By the time I came on the project, a script had already been completed by two other writers. But the director, Fritz Lang, didn't like it one bit, so my job was to do a complete rewrite on the quick. Fritz was very respectful of writers in general, and I enjoyed working with him. But he had very exacting standards of professional morality. I remember mentioning a writer, John Wexley, who had worked with him on an earlier film.

"He is a dishonest man," Fritz immediately declared. Although I wasn't particularly fond of Wexley, I knew of nothing to call his integrity into question, so I asked Fritz what he meant. "He's thoroughly dishonest," he replied. "When we worked on the script for *Hangmen Also Die*, I told him it had to be shortened by twenty pages, and he came back with a script that was twenty pages shorter; but I found that only ten pages in actual length had been cut. The rest was by his instructing his secretary to put more lines on a page!" This was a fairly common writer's offense and not exactly a crime. But Fritz was very indignant about it.

During the war, it seemed appropriate to most American Communists when the National Committee, led by Earl Browder, announced the "dissolution" of the party and the formation of a broader, more democratic Communist Political Association (C.P.A.). The change seemed only to bring the nomenclature in line with reality: Our political activities, by then, were virtually identical to those of our liberal friends. To me it had a special significance. It seemed to fit with a growing good feeling I was beginning to experience as an Allied victory appeared inevitable. That victory had been won by the two great powers in the world, one democratic, one Communist, who had found a way of working together for shared ideals, and who both realized— or so I believed—that the introduction of atomic weapons made future wars unthinkable. For all the problems that remained in the world, the defeat of fascism, with its outdated racist and nationalist myths, was the defeat of unreason. In ten or twenty years, maybe thirty at the outside, I imagined, it would be unthinkable for one people to assault another because of their national origin, for any human to regard another human as belonging to an inferior race, or for anyone of moderate intelligence and a smattering of education to question evolution or believe that God created the world a few millennia ago.

The C.P.A. had a short life. Before the end of the war, a dissenting minority in the Party, led by William Z. Foster, was fortified into a majority by a letter from Jacques Duclos, a French Communist leader, denouncing Browder's move and its theoretical foundations. Anti-Communists interpreted this as an order—we, as a strong suggestion—from the Communist International to the American Party to shape up. The hostility toward the Soviet Union already surfacing in the highest reaches of the American government made Browder's appraisal look shaky, in any case. Roosevelt had died, and Truman's record did not make him a promising successor. When Germany invaded Russia, he had publicly expressed the hope that they destroy each other. Now he was flaunting the atomic bomb as an American secret and taking his foreign policy cues from former wartime British Prime Minister Winston Churchill, whose own electorate had recently repudiated him in favor of the Labor Party.

Almost no one had anticipated how quickly the tide would turn to rightist reaction and a cold war. In 1946, there was a series of major strikes to which corporate America responded with equal or greater militancy. Elections that year produced the first Republican Congress since 1928. There was a Truman Doctrine to guard southeastern Europe from the Russians, a Truman loyalty program, and the conversion of H.U.A.C. from a temporary to a permanent body featuring (in addition to Chairman Thomas) John Rankin of Mississippi, a ranting white supremacist and anti-Semite, and Richard Nixon, his smoother California counterpart, who was careful to express his race prejudices only in private.

I was losing what remained of my illusions about Stalin and his "socialist state," yet it still seemed to me then that the Soviet leaders were more serious than ours about wanting peaceful relations. Ideological considerations aside, they had a persuasive, practical reason to be afraid of a war in which the other side had a monopoly on nuclear weapons; whereas a number of people in the West, in America in particular, thought we should threaten to or actually bomb them into submission while we had the superior power to do so.

As for the party to which I belonged, the question of converting America to socialism wasn't exactly on the agenda. In my own mind, the need to avoid another war and abolish nuclear weapons—to preserve the planet—had become more important than the particular political or economic systems we embraced. Yet I shared a growing awareness that American Communists and the left generally were going to be under attack. Already, leaders of the Joint Anti-Fascist Refugee Committee were facing prison sentences for Contempt of Congress because they had refused to turn over their records to H.U.A.C. In Hollywood, political differences were sharpened by an acrimonious labor dispute which began as a jurisdictional quarrel between the reactionary International Alliance of Theatrical Stage Employees (I.A.T.S.E.) and the progressive Conference of Studio Unions (C.S.U.), both of which belonged to the American Federation of Labor. When A.F.L. President William Green decided the issue in favor of the C.S.U., the I.A.T.S.E. and the movie studios ignored him, forcing the C.S.U. into what turned out to be a suicidal strike.

Communists and liberals who supported the strike were also in the main members of the Hollywood Independent Citizens Committee of the Arts, Sciences, and Professions (with its hard-to-swallow acronym H.I.C.C.A.S.P.), which ended up backing Henry Wallace and the Progressive Party against both Truman and Dewey in the 1948 election. In the Screen Actors Guild, the most conspicuous sympathizers with the strikers were Katharine Hepburn, Edward G. Robinson, Alexander Knox, Howard da Silva, John Garfield, Karen Morley, Paul Henreid, and Franchot Tone. The militants on the other side also had their political arm, called the Motion Picture Artists for the Preservation of American Ideals. Among the leaders of that organization were Walt Disney, Ronald Reagan, George Murphy, Adolphe Menjou, Roy Brewer of I.A.T.S.E., and the directors Sam Wood, Victor Fleming, and King Vidor. The Screen Writers Guild was split on the strike, and in 1947 progressives suffered a serious setback in Guild elections, the main question at stake being whether to require executive board members to sign "loyalty" affidavits swearing they were not Communists.

During the final year of the war in Europe, when my brother David was killed in Germany, I went to New York out of concern for my mother, who had just suffered her third tragic loss in eleven years. But I was also worried about David's wife, Frances, and their two babies. I was making a good deal of money and wanted to contribute what I could to their support. I discovered, however, that Frances was quite capable of combining motherhood with two regular radio shows and occasional theater jobs. I also found that she shared my political views and was starting to actively promote them as a way of continuing the struggle David had been writing about. Silvia and I were already leading quite separate lives. Over the next two years I made several trips to New York, and, in between, Frances and I developed a relationship by mail that became personal. In September 1946, she boarded a transcontinental train with Katie and Joe. As one of them put it, "We're going to Canyonfornia to marry Uncle Bill."

While we were on our honeymoon, I spoke by phone to a friend who warned me that a California version of H.U.A.C. had begun issuing subpoenas. I managed to duck that invitation by prolonging our trip. But soon enough, the main body in Washington announced its intention to investigate the movie business, commencing with a set of closed hearings in Los Angeles in the spring of 1947. Frances and I had just found a new home in Santa Monica, with a tennis court out back. We were getting ready to move out of a rented house nearby when a deputy United States marshal appeared at the door, and handed me a bright pink document bearing J. Parnell Thomas's signature: "By authority of the House of Representatives of the Congress of the United States of America," it said, I was "commanded to appear before the Un-American Activities Committee . . . in their chamber in the city of Washington . . . and not to depart without leave of such committee. Herein fail not . . . "

six
"None of Their Business"

IN the late summer of 1945, Darryl Zanuck asked Otto Preminger to take over the movie version of *Forever Amber*, a mildly lascivious best-seller that Fox had purchased with high commercial hopes. Otto, in turn, brought me into the project.

Otto was extremely bright and curious about almost everything. He was also very good company, and when we worked together, we tended to spend as much time talking about the world in general as we did about the movie at hand. In his native Vienna, Otto had been a theatrical prodigy, invited at seventeen to join the Josefstadt Theater under the illustrious Max Reinhardt, and, at twenty-six, to succeed him as artistic director. The main thing he had gained from his early years as an actor, it sometimes seemed, was complete scorn for the profession. Young performers, in particular, saw Otto at his most terrifying. On a crowded set, he would abruptly discontinue a take to tell an actor that he was doing it all wrong; then, in a louder and angrier voice, that he didn't seem to have the slightest idea what the scene was about; and finally, in a furious rant, that he was trying to *sabotage* the picture. My name for this cycle of mounting rage was "Otto-intoxication." The first time I mentioned it to him, Otto was offended. Later he decided to be amused.

Fresh off the success of *Laura*, Otto was grateful for my covert contributions to that picture, which had put him in Fox's good graces after an earlier association that had led Zanuck to declare that Otto would never direct for the studio again. On *Forever Amber*, a script had already been completed by Philip Dunne, who, among his other credits, had written one of the most distinguished movies of the 1940s, *How Green Was My Valley*. (With that picture, he had pulled off the remarkable feat of getting Zanuck and Fox to tell a story that made a powerful case for labor unions.) I was now supposed to collaborate with Phil on a rewrite—a touchy situation, or, rather, it would have been if he had been any less of an exemplar of graciousness and professionalism. As it was, the three of us, Otto, Phil, and I, established a strong bond based, in part, on a fervent common desire to be working on almost any property other than the one Zanuck had foisted on us.

Notwithstanding these sentiments, we hammered together a script that led Zanuck to once again offer me a long-term contract. The starting salary was $2000 a week—high pay for a young screenwriter in those days. I signed, however, less for the money than for the protection a studio deal might provide against the political trouble I saw coming. In fact, Fox seemed less fearful than the other studios, and Zanuck, despite his fondness for polo and big-game hunting, had a weakness for movies dealing with difficult social issues; it was this lone non-Jew among the moguls who tackled anti-Semitism when Sam Goldwyn wouldn't; from that topic, he moved on to racism with *Pinky*, and fired his old friend John Ford after the first rushes convinced him of the need for a director who was more advanced in his thinking. ("Ford's Negroes were like Aunt Jemima," Zanuck said later. "Caricatures.") He hired Elia Kazan to direct the picture instead.

For my first screenplay as a Fox contract writer, I selected a novel about the British upper class called *Britannia Mews*. (The studio gave the movie a different title, *The Forbidden Street*.) I was working on final revisions when the subpoena came.

The Committee had chosen nineteen of us as personifications of the threat it was out to expose. *The Hollywood Reporter* dubbed us "the unfriendly nineteen," to distinguish us from the "friendly" witnesses who had appeared at closed hearings the previous spring and would now simply be repeating their testimony in public. One of the nineteen, the great German playwright Bertolt Brecht, had been under supervision as an enemy alien during the war, and the invitation to appear before H.U.A.C. merely reinforced his desire to leave America as soon as possible. With that object in mind, Brecht obtained separate counsel and opted not to join the rest of us in a series of meetings where we plotted legal strategy.

The big question facing us was how to respond to the inevitable "Are you now or have you ever been a member of the Communist Party?" Some of the group wanted to affirm their membership, while a few were eager to declare for all the world that they had never been party members. But Trumbo and I, who had considered the problem in detail, argued that the only satisfactory answer was no answer. If you had been a communist and said so, the next demand would be for the names of other party members, and you had less of a constitutional case for refusing to discuss others' political activities than

Ring, Jr. at two

Frances Chaney (Lardner) publicity still mid-forties

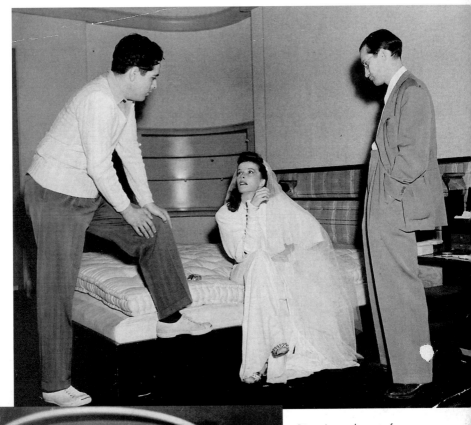

Ring, Jr. on the set of
Woman of the Year with
Katharine Hepburn and
co-author Michael Kanin, 1941

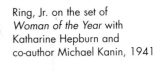

Ring, Jr. and Otto Preminger
arriving in Rome, 1963

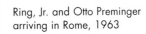

Cannes Film Festival,
1970 Grand Prix to M*A*S*H.
L to R: Jo Ann Pflug, actress; Ring Lardner, Jr.,
screenplay writer; Robert Altman, director;
Ingo Preminger, producer; Sally Kellerman,
actress

Ring, Jr. with Muhammad Ali on the set of
The Greatest / *The Miami Herald*

Ring, Jr. at 1947 HUAC hearings / UPI / Corbis-Bettmann

Dalton Trumbo early 1940s / Cleo Trumbo

Ring, Jr. prison photograph

Hugo Butler at Trumbo Ranch mid-forties

Ian Hunter, 1979

Paul Jarrico, 1997 / Jilly Wendell

Ring, Jr. with Sylvia Jarrico at the
Abe Polanski memorial, 1999
Bob Carey / The Los Angeles Times

your own. If you weren't a Communist, saying so conceded the Committee's right to ask the question in the first place. We talked about the possibility of invoking Fifth Amendment protection against self-incrimination; but that, we decided, would be tantamount to admitting that party membership was a crime. (The government itself had not yet alleged that it was. Prosecutions of party leaders under the Smith Act began a year later.)

Trumbo and I wanted to make a First Amendment issue of the committee's right to inquire into our beliefs and associations. Taking such a stand meant risking prosecution for Contempt of Congress, a little-known and rarely enforced "statutory" misdemeanor, which carried a maximum sentence of a year in prison. But there was reason to believe that the judiciary might be sympathetic to our position. In several earlier cases, the Supreme Court had indicated that since movies came under the freedom of the press clause, Congress had no right to legislate their content, and where it could not legislate, it had no right to investigate. Declining to answer on First Amendment grounds seemed to hold an additional advantage: If we won in the courts, the Committee might soon be out of business.

After discussion, the eighteen of us who were U.S. citizens agreed to take this common approach. Then one of our lawyers, with the best of intentions, threw a monkey wrench into our plans. "If we end up in the courts, I wouldn't trust most of our Federal judges," was the gist of his advice. "I would ask for a jury trial because I believe an American jury would want to acquit you if they had grounds for doing so. But they'd have to accept all the Constitutional doctrine in the judge's instructions, and the grounds would have to be an issue of fact. So I want you not to refuse to answer a question but say you're trying to answer it in your own way." The lawyer in question, Robert Kenny, was a former Attorney General of California, and the rest of our legal team made the grave mistake of going along with his ploy, which accomplished nothing in the end except to make us seem weaselly and abrasive in the eyes of some liberals who supported our position but not our way of expressing it. Many of them said at the time what most of us later concluded ourselves: If the idea was to challenge the Committee's right to ask such questions, a simple and straightforward refusal would have been a more dignified and effective way to make the point.

The Committee devoted the first week of its hearings to the "friendly" witnesses. The Russian-born novelist Ayn Rand, whose book *The Fountainhead* was already a right-wing favorite in this country, testified that she had never once seen a smiling child in the Soviet Union from the time of the Revolution in 1917 until her departure in 1926. The others focused on the enormity of the Red menace in Hollywood. Gary Cooper said he had turned down a number of scripts that were "tinged with Communist ideas." In a similar vein, Jack Warner recalled his tireless efforts, as vice president in charge of production at Warner Brothers, to keep writers from sneaking what he called "stuff" into the studio product. As an example, he cited a line of dialogue he had eliminated from Clifford Odets's script for a movie called *Humoresque.* Except for his vigilance, Warner testified, the American people might have been subjected to the experience of listening to John Garfield tell Joan Crawford: "Your father is a banker. My father lives over a grocery store."

In the thirties, Warners had been known for the gritty realism of movies like *I Was a Prisoner on a Chain Gang.* In the rash of strikes that broke out after the war, however, Warner operatives had directed tear gas bombs and high-pressure fire hoses at picketing workers, and Jack Warner had publicly declared that he was through with pictures about "the little man." Nevertheless, as he told the committee, he had qualms about firing writers merely on the basis of their reported political affiliations or activities. The studios, he suggested, would be sitting ducks, legally, if they followed such a course.

Louis B. Mayer, who testified later, was also nervous about a *private* blacklist; precisely because the studios might be breaking the law by organizing a purge on their own, though, Mayer entreated Congress to do the job for them. He called for "legislation establishing a national policy regulating employment of Communists in private industry." In adopting such a policy, he suggested, America would merely be denying them "the sanctuary of the freedom they seek to destroy."

When the "unfriendlies' " turn came, Trumbo, the most commercially successful of us, lugged a stack of scripts to the witness stand with him and demanded that the Committee point to a single instance of Communist propaganda. Ginger Rogers's mother Lela had actually made such an accusation against Trumbo, citing a line he had written for her daughter in a wartime tearjerker called *Tender Comrade*: "Share and share alike, that's democracy." Chairman Thomas, however, declined to pursue that line of inquiry, insisting that he and his colleagues had no interest in anything as un-American as censorship. Just the previous week, the president of the Association of Motion Picture Producers, Eric Johnston, had assured our lawyers that his organization would never contemplate anything as un-American as a blacklist.

Ten of us had been given definite appearance dates in their subpoenas; eight, of whom I was one, had been instructed to wait at home until dates were assigned. In a show of solidarity, however, we decided to travel together, making public appeals for support en route and in Washington; and after a photo of Frances and me sitting in the audience appeared prominently in a newspaper, I was abruptly called to the stand on what turned out to be the last day of the hearings, replacing my friend Waldo Salt. Ironically, our inability to plead self-incrimination led the ten of us to become convicts. When the Committee got around to holding its next round of Hollywood hearings, in 1951, none of the witnesses had to suffer that fate. By then, the leaders of the American Communist Party were in prison, convicted under the Smith Act of advocating the violent overthrow of the government. Thus Waldo and many other witnesses could escape criminal charges by taking the Fifth. But that didn't stop M.G.M. from firing Waldo the minute the hearings ended. For the later witnesses, as for us, there was no way to avoid the blacklist except to admit you had been a Communist and then to dramatize your repentance by naming all the other party members you could think of.

Bertolt Brecht, soon to depart for what was now East Germany, also appeared on that final day of the 1947 hearings. "Looking back at my experiences as a playwright and poet in the Europe of the last two decades," he testified, "I wish to say that the great American people would lose much and risk much if they allowed anybody to restrict free competition of ideas in cultural fields, or to interfere with art which must be free to be art." As a "guest in this country," however, he offered to tell the Committee anything it wanted to know about him personally. He had never been a Communist, he said, and had deliberately avoided all forms of political activity during his time in the U.S. As for the "revolutionary" works cited by the Committee counsel, Robert Stripling, Brecht gently reminded the Committee that they had been written as part of "the fight against Hitler," whose government was the only one he had ever sought to overthrow. For Stripling, however, and for at least a few of the Committee members as well, even anti-Nazi activity was now suspect. It was a sign of just how far the political mood had shifted since the end of the war.

The day ended with a "surprise" witness—a former F.B.I. agent named Louis Russell, who told an involved tale about how a professor named Haakon Chevalier had supposedly pumped his friend

Robert Oppenheimer for information about the atomic bomb, with the intention, so Russell alleged, of passing it on to foreign agents. Chevalier wrote an entire book to demonstrate that this was non-sense, and, true or false, the story didn't have much to do with the movie business, despite Russell's attempts to establish such a con-nection by citing some minor social contacts between Chevalier and a couple of the unfriendly witnesses. So farfetched, indeed, did the idea of a link between Hollywood and Soviet spying and sabotage seem that most of the newspapers largely ignored the testimony. But one, the tabloid *New York Daily News*, took it seriously enough to run, next to a large picture of me leaving the witness stand, this screaming headline:

RED QUIZ BARES
ATOM SPY PLOT

It was hardly the sort of publicity likely to reassure the studio bosses, to say nothing of respectable relatives on both my mother's and father's side of the family. My mother herself respected my polit-ical beliefs, even if she didn't agree with them, and she never sus-pected me of being a spy. Still grieving for two dead sons, however, she feared that I was in for a rough time.

So did I.

The press coverage of the hearings was massive, lending weight to our suspicion that it was the lure of publicity that had drawn the Committee's attention to Hollywood in the first place. What with the array of movie star witnesses during the first week of hearings and the lineup of additional celebrities, including Humphrey Bogart, Lauren Bacall, Groucho Marx, Frank Sinatra, and Danny Kaye, who arrived the following week to condemn the investigation under the banner of a group called the Committee for the First Amendment, we made front pages across the country. But this was so early in the era of McCarthyism that Joe McCarthy himself had not yet discovered the virtues of witch-hunting. Columnists and editorial writers for some of the nation's more respectable newspapers vocally disapproved of the Committee's program and methods, and there was reason to think that the sudden suspension of the hearings, with a number of the unfriendly witnesses as yet uncalled, was designed to ward off more such adverse reaction. Nevertheless, I had an uneasy feeling that we were fighting a losing battle.

Because the producer was in a hurry for *The Forbidden Street*, I had promised to do the finishing touches on the Washington trip, during which I remained on salary. After I turned in the script, the studio had the contractual right to invoke a layoff period in which I would be off salary, or it could give me another assignment. Fox chose the latter course because Preminger had bought a book he wanted me to adapt.

A month after the hearings, Mr. Johnston's M.P.P.A. met at the Waldorf Astoria Hotel in New York. It was a gathering dominated by the more conservative banker types at the head of the parent organizations in the East rather than the Hollywood executives engaged in actual movie production. They passed a resolution declaring that they would no longer employ any of the Ten or anyone else who took a similar stand. Five of us were on studio payrolls at the time, Adrian Scott and I under long-term contract.

I was in the middle of a conference with Otto when his secretary came in to say that Mr. Lardner was to report to Mr. Zanuck's office. *"Only* Mr. Lardner?" Otto asked, almost incredulous at the affront to his dignity as a producer-director. I reminded him that Zanuck might have something else on his mind besides our project. And I was right. My instructions were to proceed not to Zanuck's inner sanctum but to the office of the studio manager, who told me to quit the premises immediately and not come back. Zanuck had said earlier that he wouldn't fire anybody (by which he meant me, since I was the only member of the Ten at Fox) unless ordered to by his board of directors. The board had swiftly obliged him.

When I stopped in the writers' building to collect my things, two of the studio's most esteemed employees, my friend Phil Dunne and the writer-director George Seaton, offered to walk out with me in protest. I persuaded them that any effective countermove would have to be on a much grander scale. Phil was, like me, the son of a famous writer—Finley Peter Dunne—known for using the vernacular to humorous effect. We had become friends, and years later, in his autobiography, he recalled receiving pretty much the same advice from me that he got from Zanuck. "Don't do anything foolish," was what we both basically told him. In retrospect, Phil added, he wished he had defied us both.

Twelve years would pass before any of the major studios knowingly let me in the door again. (But R.K.O., unknowingly, sanctioned one visit. A producer who happened to be a Princeton alumnus decided to invite the entire Princeton Club of southern California to a showing of his latest picture. Membership in that chapter of the club encompassed everyone in the region who had put in any time at Princeton. The producer was startled, to say the least, when I showed up.)

Frances, the children, and I continued to live in our large new house as long as there was any hope of winning in the courts. After the House of Representatives as a whole cited the Ten for contempt, we were indicted by a Federal grand jury, and the first two of us, John Howard Lawson and Dalton Trumbo, went on trial in Washington, were convicted, and received sentences of a year in prison. To avoid the expense of eight more trials, the rest of us had agreed to abide by the law established in these pilot cases. If Trumbo and Lawson won their appeal, we would all be free; if they lost, we faced nothing more than a perfunctory trial and sentencing.

During this limbo period, a number of independent producers continued to employ us anonymously. Some hoped to see us vindicated and restored to respectability; others merely relished the prospect of getting our services at reduced rates. Regardless of motivation, these jobs paid only a quarter to a third of our normal wages, and the hush-hush nature of the business dealings gave me a first taste of what it might actually have been like to be a spy. Among the sympathizers were actors Burgess Meredith and Franchot Tone, who engaged me to work on an adaptation of a John Steinbeck story called *Shark Wicks*. Although they never got the financial backing to make the picture, Franchot and I had a clandestine meeting at his bank where he handed me ten thousand dollars in cash.

Otto Preminger's brother, Ingo, a theatrical agent, took me on as a client at this unpromising juncture. Like the other members of the Ten, I had been, in effect, fired by my representatives at the William Morris Agency, which was just one of a number of ancillary Hollywood institutions that might have resisted the blacklist but aided it instead. In 1949, Ingo put me in touch with Lazar Wechsler, a Swiss producer who was preparing to make an English-language picture called *Four Days Leave*, starring Cornel Wilde. He was under contract to Fox, which had released *The Forbidden Street* with my name as sole screenplay author, and the brass now agreed to lend Wilde to Wechsler on the assurance that I would be writing "the English dialogues." The indirect compliment didn't quite compensate for my abrupt expulsion from the premises.

Since Wechsler was in a hurry, I flew from Santa Monica to Washington to arrange a passport. The man who took my application disappeared for an ominously long time. On his return, he informed me that "Mrs. Shipley"—this was Ruth Shipley, the then-director of the passport bureau and known as a conservative—"wants you to be aware, Mr. Lardner, that the State Department has no objection whatsoever to your travel wherever you wish to go." Adrian Scott and Edward Dmytryk had already gotten permission to work abroad. But their passports, unlike mine, had been limited to England, France, and Switzerland—an omen of tighter travel restrictions to come.

The director of the movie, Leopold Lindtberg, was Austrian, and he needed a dialogue director to help two young French actresses, Josette Day and Simone Signoret, perform in English. I convinced Wechsler that Frances would be ideal for the job, and he arranged for her transportation to Geneva. Living up to my advance billing, she worked hard and became close with both actresses, Simone especially. Frances even played a bit part in the movie herself.

Trumbo and Lawson's appeal was turned down, and in May 1950 the Supreme Court announced that it would not reexamine the decision. Four votes had been needed; only two were available. It was the kind of case, legal experts agreed, in which it might have been difficult for the Court to decide against us in view of past precedents. The experts also agreed that the Court sometimes ducked a controversial issue this way. Deciding a nearly identical case years later, the Warren Court seemed to say we had been right all along—small consolation for imprisonment and a fifteen-year blacklist.

By the time of the Court's rebuff in 1950, the atmosphere around the country had become even more chilling. McCarthy had appeared clutching his invisible list of Communists in the State Department; Julius and Ethel Rosenberg had been sentenced to the electric chair for stealing atomic secrets for the Soviets; and across the Pacific, in a country that few Americans had even heard of, the Cold War was about to turn hot. While Lawson and Trumbo began to serve their sentences in 1950, the remainder of the Ten were given their ceremonial trials in pairs before two different judges. Albert Maltz and I appeared together. The judge listened to Martin Popper, our Washington lawyer, for a few minutes, then pronounced us guilty but postponed sentencing for a week.

It was a notable week: The Korean War broke out and Truman sent American troops into action. When we returned from some money-raising efforts in New York and Long Island, Maltz's case came first, and Popper made a pre-sentencing speech about Albert's civic contributions. The judge was impressed. He hadn't realized what a distinguished citizen the defendant was, he said; now that he did, he felt all the more obliged to give him the maximum allowable sentence—one year—as a lesson to others. I whispered to Popper that he could skip any recital of my civic merits. But I, too, was sentenced to a year, as were the four others who appeared before that jurist. The directors Edward Dmytryk and Herbert Biberman were sentenced by a different judge who decided that their misconduct deserved only six months.

Samuel Ornitz, the oldest of the Ten, had a heart problem and went to the medical center for Federal prisoners, while Adrian Scott's case was postponed for a short time because of illness. The other six of us began to serve our sentences, as Lawson and Trumbo had, at the District of Columbia Department of Corrections facility in downtown Washington—the D.C.D.C., as it was known—while awaiting assignment elsewhere. Bob Kenny, the best-connected of our lawyers, knew James Bennett, the head of the Federal Bureau of Prisons. Kenny put in a request to have us sent to an institution within visiting range of our families in Los Angeles. Bennett explained that no more than a couple of us could serve our time in the same place (the implication being that larger concentrations of Hollywood Communists might prove dangerous), and facilities in the West were ruled out because of the cost of transportation. The single concession he offered was to send me and another screenwriter, Lester Cole, to the Federal Correctional Institution (or F.C.I.) in Danbury, Connecticut, where both of us had mothers living nearby.

During the couple of weeks that we remained in Washington, the daily exercise hour gave us a chance to see and talk to one other. I had a number of conversations there with Eddie Dmytryk, whom I had not known before. He was a talented director and a likable man who often came up with an insider's view of the big news of the day, as if he had a secret, highly placed contact whispering in his ear. After what most of the world took for an invasion of South Korea by North Korea, Eddie privately advised me that South Korea was the true attacker, acting at the instigation of John Foster Dulles, our then Secretary of State.

Lester and I went to Danbury by train, each handcuffed to a U.S. Marshal, neither of whom, it developed, had made the journey before. They had been instructed to change to a northbound train at Norwalk. As we approached the South Norwalk station, I told them that I knew the route well from my many trips to New Milford, where my mother lived, and that Norwalk and South Norwalk were one and the same. They were so skeptical of my information that we almost failed to get off the train in time. When we did, the marshals were equally reluctant to accept my advice about where to find the connecting train. In the end, however, I brought us successfully to Danbury, where we were met by a car from the F.C.I.

My first glimpse of my new home-away-from-home was from the bottom of a steep, winding driveway. At that angle, the square stone prison building seemed to overwhelm the hilltop; later I discovered a considerable tract of level acreage at its rear, every square foot devoted to some farming purpose—vegetable plots, fruit trees, a chicken yard, milk cows, pigs, rabbits, and other edible animals. Most of the food served at our meals came from this inmate-tended farm.

The D.C.D.C. had been interesting: It was the only penal institution in the country that housed both Federal prisoners and local offenders, including pickpockets and heavy-duty drunks who were rounded up in the streets and confined overnight. The Danbury clientele was more homogeneous. The place served as a kind of halfway house for a handful of serious street criminals who were nearing release after serving long penitentiary terms; otherwise, almost all of us had been convicted of white-collar crimes, which included mail theft, crossing a state line with a stolen automobile, defrauding the military on wartime contracts, draft evasion (or, in some cases, conscientious objection on the part of young men lacking the proper religious credentials), bribery of Internal Revenue Service agents, and spying for the enemy during World War II.

A single inmate already there had been charged with our particular offense. Jacob Auslander, M.D., had fallen victim to H.U.A.C. in the Joint Anti-Fascist Refugee Committee case. The F.C.I. administration had assigned him to assist the prison's civilian M.D., and it was he who gave me the physical required of every new prisoner. Jake completed his term soon after we began ours. Some months later, however, I overheard a young inmate telling a new arrival about the inmate doctor who had examined him.

"A real doctor?" replied his listener in disbelief. "What was he in for?"

"I don't know—drugs, I guess."

Feeling called upon to defend Jake's reputation, I briefly explained the work of the Refugee Committee and the reasons for its refusal to turn over a list of the people it had helped get out of Franco's Spain. My fellow inmates listened with what seemed like respectful attention. Then the veteran spoke in a polite tone: "Well, I guess it was some of that and drugs, too."

There was a similar lack of understanding about the crime that had put Lester and me in Danbury, but it was assumed to have been some kind of refusal to talk to the cops, and for that we received general approval. As for the experience of being a jailbird, I have never gone so far as to actually recommend it. Prison does expand your social contacts, however. It is also possible to find behind bars the sort of serenity that T.E. Lawrence experienced as Aircraftman Shaw—the peace of mind that comes with freedom from responsibility. You can't get it by some form of voluntary retreat, terminable at your option. The element of choice must be removed. But as soon as it's clear that you can't do anything about anything, you're free to think about whatever comes into your mind. In Danbury, I was able to focus on a single line of thought with a concentration I have never been able to muster since.

Ever since my days as a convict, I have urged anyone considering a career as a law-breaker to stick to breaking Federal ones, since the accommodations are so measurably superior to those at state or local jails. Danbury offered edible if not elegant food, much of it farm-grown by prisoners like Lester Cole and J. Parnell Thomas, who enjoyed minimum-security status. ("Still handling the chicken shit, I see," said the former, greeting the latter at the poultry yard where he performed his labors.)

The quantitative difference between a one-year sentence and a longer one carries with it a qualitative difference, as well. The shorter term seems but a temporary inconvenience. As you begin it, you are already counting the days until it will be over, so you don't feel the frustration and self-pity that goes with a more sustained confinement.

Most of the housing at Danbury was in large dormitory rooms with individual cubicles containing a cot and a table with a couple of drawers. But there were a small number of individual cells for inmates whose jobs involved abnormal working hours. During my initial weeks in a dormitory setting, I was troubled with insomnia, so

I applied for the single-cell housing on the grounds that I was falling asleep at my typewriter. Though most of my fellow prisoners didn't like the cells because they were locked up at night, I found sleeping there easier and the rarely interrupted silence more congenial to reading and writing. One of the few interruptions I remember, beyond the regular prison count, was from an inmate who came to the bars of my cell and asked if I could please spare a moment to give him some advice. He was nearing release and had been told that I was from Hollywood. What he wanted to know was, "Do they go for the main line out there? I heard you can get a couple of hundred dollars an ounce."

I asked him how that compared with prices in New York.

"New York! Shit, man, nobody works New York no more! The laws they got there, you can get ten or fifteen years for a first sale."

I had to tell him that I had no solid information about the market for heroin in my adopted hometown.

Those of us with one-year sentences were technically eligible for parole after eight months. While we didn't expect it to be granted in that hysterical year, we went through the formality of asking our wives to solicit letters of support that could be filed with our parole applications. In my case, the letters included one from Kate Hepburn, sent by her directly to me in Danbury; I was especially appreciative, since Kate must have realized the attention that her name would arouse in the censorship process. When I saw her again for the first time thirteen years later, she waved off my thanks in characteristically brisk fashion. "I don't think I ever did such a thing," she insisted. "I'd remember it if I had."

Frances was able to make only one cross-country trip to visit me in Danbury. Among other things, she reported that Joe, our six-year-old, had been asked by another first-grader why his Daddy was in jail. "My Daddy's in jail," he replied, "because some guy in

Washington asked him a question that was none of their business, and my Daddy told him it was none of their business, and it is none of their business."

With his six-month sentence, Eddie Dmytryk was not eligible for parole, but he got a month off for good behavior. Then, in mid-November, we read a newspaper story about a statement he had made on his release, declaring that he had left the Party some years back. The event that had turned him into an anti-Communist, he said, was the unwarranted and vicious attack by the North Koreans on their peace-loving neighbors to the south. He had refrained from announcing his conversion in prison lest it be taken as a subterfuge to reduce his jail time. Now he could reveal himself as a true American and hope to be able to resume his life's work in the movies.

The news of his transformation reminded me, of course, of Eddie's discourse on the origins of the Korean War while in the D.C.D.C. I also recalled another observation that he had made during our legal battle. "You know," he had in effect said, "it's really more remarkable for me to have stuck with this thing this long than for you writers who can work under the table, which a director can't do. I've never directed anything on the stage. I've never done anything but movies, first as a cutter and then as a director."

Another interruption of my peace in that single cell occurred shortly before my release at the beginning of April 1951. An inmate I knew only casually came to my door in a whirl of excitement. "Hey, they're talking about you on the radio!" he exclaimed. I followed him to the common room, where a news broadcast was in progress, little noticed by the other prisoners in earshot. H.U.A.C., now under a new chairman, was once again investigating Communist infiltration of the movie business. The witness on the stand, reciting a long list of names of his former comrades, including me, was my old friend

Richard Collins. A long parade of witnesses testified in a series of public sessions that year, and hundreds of men and women were added to the blacklist. Some had been named and had failed to clear themselves to the Committee's satisfaction. Others, the first witnesses to be guided by our experience and the Smith Act convictions, invoked the Fifth Amendment. It kept them out of prison but, from a career standpoint, was no better than the First.

Collins was only the first of many cooperative witnesses to claim that he had been careful not to cause any personal harm with his testimony. His rule of thumb, he explained, was to identify only those who had been called previously as unfriendly witnesses, like the Ten; those who had already been named as communists; and those who had left the party so long ago that, he reasoned, no one would hold their membership against them. Among this last group, however, was my old friend Budd Schulberg, who, seeing his former political activities discussed on the front page of the *New York Times,* was understandably concerned. Although Budd was not working in Hollywood at the time (he had just completed a novel, *The Disenchanted,* about a writer modeled on Scott Fitzgerald), he felt an urgent need to "clear" himself. His method of doing so was an appearance before the committee in which he saluted its work, went on at some length about the domestic as well as global communist menace, and named some names of his own.

Budd, too, had a theory about just which of his old friends were beyond further harm. So did the director Elia Kazan, another volunteer-witness who insisted on testifying after demonstrating his ability to make a living in a field (the legitimate theatre) where his employment was not in jeopardy. And yet, as Victor Navasky has pointed out in his book on the blacklist (*Naming Names*), being fingered once wasn't necessarily as bad for someone's career as having it happen three times or six times; in any case, Schulberg and Kazan (and this, too, was a recurring pattern) didn't quite manage to adhere to their own guidelines. Both added fresh names to the public record despite their insistence that they hadn't.

Although I was not permitted to use a prison typewriter for my own work, I was free to write with a pencil and pad, and I began work on a novel, *The Ecstasy of Owen Muir*. I had persuaded my custodians that with the movie business closed to me, my best professional prospects lay in fiction. I also felt free to confide the subject matter of the book I was writing: It was to be about a Roman Catholic marriage. (I saw no point in adding that my intentions were satirical.) For this commendable purpose, the prison authorities let Frances send me packages of handwritten notes and several books on Roman Catholic doctrine.

The clerk in charge of me was a devout Catholic, as it happened. Impressed by the official church imprimatur on these shipments, he advised the Catholic chaplain that one of the Red-hots was showing signs of going their way. The result was an invitation to midnight mass on Christmas Eve, which I accepted. I did so not only because it seemed politic but because I was planning a midnight mass scene in the book. A few days later, the clerk brought me to a meeting with the chaplain for the purpose, it soon became clear, of satisfying my obvious desire to join their faith. Luckily, I had anticipated this. Were I to feel ready to make such a drastic switch, I replied, doing so under conditions of duress might be construed as a trick to gain sympathy and possible parole. It was essentially the same argument Dmytryk had used a few weeks before.

The idea for the book had come from my curiosity about the ways in which a few Catholic acquaintances had bypassed official doctrine on matters like virginity, contraception, divorce, abortion, and mandatory devotions. Born into Catholic families and baptized by the Church, they regarded themselves as part of that faith for life and knew that no matter how far they strayed from its rules and rituals, they could always get a blanket absolution from a priest administering last rites. What, I wondered, if I matched such a nominal Catholic with an idealistic and utterly sincere convert?

From a professional-rehabilitation standpoint, I had made an unfortunate choice of subject matter. Two years after my release from prison, I began to submit the completed manuscript to publishers. In England, I had swift success, landing a deal with the eminent firm of Jonathan Cape, Ltd. Feeling it prudent to prepare them for the dark suspicions that my name was likely to arouse in my native land, I sent them a cautionary letter. The reply, from Mr. Cape himself, dimissed the H.U.A.C. investigation as a "curious affair" that might be a useful publicity angle. That, alas, was not how American publishers seemed to view it. The manuscript drew gratifying reactions from editors at several major houses, only to be rejected in the end by their superiors. Undoubtedly, the fact that this was the zenith moment of what has come to be called the McCarthy Era had its effect. One editor told me in confidence, however, that what killed the book at his firm was fear of the Catholic Church and the possibility of losing the parochial-school market for the firm's textbooks. In the end, I had to settle for Cameron and Kahn, a left-wing publishing house headed by Angus Cameron, who had himself run afoul of H.U.A.C., losing his job at Little, Brown. His new outfit occupied a marginal place in the publishing world, and most of the major newspapers and magazines simply ignored the book until a new edition appeared, under more mainstream auspices, some fifteen years later. Still more recently, in 1997, I had the gratification of seeing it republished in a "Literary Classics" series along with works by Twain, Chekhov, Hawthorne, and Aristophanes. But at the time, the reception made it apparent that book-writing was not going to be the road back to solvency or professional security.

It was a panic-stricken Hollywood to which nine of the Hollywood Ten, released from prison that spring of 1951, returned. Even for Dmytryk, the way was not entirely clear. He wanted to re-establish himself in a dignified manner by speaking only of his own political views, but when he tried that in one Committee appearance, he found he still couldn't get a job. Then, overcoming any last, vestigial scruples, he named a long list of fellow Party members, including a couple of directors who had arrived in Hollywood after the date he gave for leaving the Party himself.

For the rest of us, the under-the-table script market had all but vanished. Many people were afraid even to speak to us, although I managed to land one job, working for the director Joseph Losey on *The Big Night*, his last American picture before he exiled himself to England for the rest of his life. He had already hired Frances as dialogue director and our friend Hugo Butler had started to rewrite the script while it was being shot. When Hugo heard that a subpoena was out for him, he moved to Mexico with his large family, and Joe asked me to take over, paying me a modest wage out of his own pocket. It was my last American movie job for eight years.

Within a year of our release, the Butlers were joined in Mexico by the Trumbos, the Maltzes, the Kahns, the Hunters, the Peppers, and the Lardners. For most of us, Mexico was just a way-station while we came to terms with the blacklist. But Hugo and George Pepper remained there for much of the next two decades and became active in the Mexican movie industry, forming a production partnership with the great Spanish director Luis Bunuel—also banished for political reasons from his native land.

Frances had a little money left from David's life insurance, and we lived on that while I worked on *Owen Muir*. Silvia, establishing herself in the construction business in Orange County, California, voluntarily waived all legal claims stemming from our divorce settlement, and supported Peter and Ann herself until I was making enough money to help in their college years. Even so, we didn't have the wherewithal to subsidize the long process of writing a book. After a pleasant six months in Mexico, we moved in on my mother in Connecticut, and Frances, fortunately, was able to find work in New York.

Mother's house was only about fifteen miles from the Danbury FCI, where she had come to see me as often as was permissible. On those trips to the prison visiting room, it had been difficult to tell how my situation affected her. She never said a word on the subject. The day I was released, she came with her chauffeur–gardener–handyman, and they drove me to my older brother's apartment in New York. That night, at home in New Milford, she suffered a stroke, which was followed by another less than a year later. Yet another year had now passed, and her doctor thought she might benefit from the presence of family in the house. Of course, three children, ages nine, eight, and three, probably wasn't what he had in mind. Still, it was the kids and her feeling of obligation not to inflict her sense of doom on them that began to restore her to something more like her former good spirits. After dinner, she would retire upstairs, and Katie, Joe, and eventually Jim would sometimes spend their last hour before going to their beds sprawled on hers, drawing stories from her about her girlhood in Indiana at the turn of the century.

In New Milford, while I finished my novel, Frances went looking for work in the theater and television. We needed the money as much as she needed the stimulation and sense of self-fulfillment, and things went well for her at first. Television, live from New York, was in what has since become known as its "golden age," and many of the people making it happen were men and women with whom Frances had worked during her highly successful years in radio. A couple of months after we returned, she was cast in a leading role on one of the most prestigious shows on the air, the Philco TV

Playhouse. After her appearance in "Holiday Song," a teleplay by Paddy Chayevsky timed for the Jewish high holidays, the producer, Fred Coe, enclosed a note with her paycheck: "You are now an official member of the Philco Playhouse." Soon she learned that Chayevsky was writing another script with a similar—but bigger—part for her.

That second show was called *Marty*. Everyone involved except Coe himself told Frances she was set for the role, and her agent secured an oral commitment from the business office for a fifty percent raise. Then, abruptly, she heard that Coe had cast another actress. He had done so without consulting anyone else in the organization, and when Frances asked for an appointment, she was informed that Coe was unable to see her. She and her agent reluctantly accepted this version of events until they began to find doors closed elsewhere in the television world. Though her own political activities, if known, might have resulted in blacklisting, her name had not appeared in *Red Channels*, the infamous publication purporting to expose communists in broadcasting; nor had she been named in anyone's Committee testimony. She had, it seemed, acquired unemployability by marriage.

Suspicion became certainty when Philco revived "Holiday Song" for the Jewish holidays the following fall. The other members of the original cast were so shocked to see Frances replaced that they threatened to strike in her behalf. Coe persuaded them it would accomplish nothing but the loss of their own jobs. Not long after that, he finally gave Frances an appointment and told her the truth, which obviously distressed him. He had tried to fight the same issue over another actor—a better-known one—and had found the network unshakable. Though she managed to land jobs in the theater, and served as an understudy for Maureen Stapleton, Claudette Colbert, and Kim Stanley, a whole decade passed before she could work in television again.

In 1954, after we had stayed with my mother for two years, a widowed younger sister of hers moved in to help take care of her and we found an apartment in New York. The following year, having finished my book, I needed work that was more immediately and predictably remunerative, and a producer named Hannah Weinstein came through for me, as she did for many others. Hannah, the former executive secretary of the leftish Independent Citizen Committee of the Arts, Sciences, and Professions, was living in England and running a TV production company. Her first project was a series starring Boris Karloff and written by the blacklisted team of Abraham Polonsky and Walter Bernstein; only moderately successful, it was not renewed for a second year. Now she had another venture in mind, for which she approached me and Ian Hunter.

Named first by Martin Berkeley and later by the director Robert Rossen, Ian had followed the same path from Hollywood to Mexico to the Upper West Side of Manhattan, where a substantial cross-industry community of blacklist victims eventually congregated. Ian and Alice, along with Zero and Kate Mostel, wound up in the same building, the Belnord, at Eighty-Sixth and Broadway. We found an apartment a few blocks uptown, at Eighty-ninth and West End.

In 1953, Ian had won an Oscar for "Roman Holiday," the last picture he worked on before the blacklist got him. Winning that award was far from an unalloyed pleasure. Ian got involved only by agreeing to front for the already-blacklisted Trumbo. It was he who had come up with the idea of a movie about a reporter and a princess on the loose in Rome. Paramount paid $50,000 for what it assumed to be Ian's (but was really Trumbo's) first draft, and hired him to do a rewrite. After Ian, too, became unemployable, several more writers were put to work on it. The result, much to Ian's (and Trumbo's) surprise, was a wonderful movie, starring Gregory Peck and the unknown Audrey Hepburn. But when Ian's name was called at the

Oscar ceremonies, it was not for the screenplay, on which he shared credit with John Dighton, but for the story, which was all Trumbo's.

Now, a year later, he seemed to have left the movie business far behind him. Since his move to New York, he had been doing public relations work for the newly formed Diners Club—it was the only job he could get. Like me, therefore, Ian was grateful to have a writing job of any kind. We were grateful, as well, to find that Hannah had chosen, for our maiden effort in the new medium, a literary property filled with stimulating possibilities. Set in medieval England and filmed largely in and around Hannah's appropriately historic estate, Foxwarren, outside London, *The Adventures of Robin Hood* gave us plenty of opportunities for oblique social comment on the issues and institutions of Eisenhower–era America. And the series was a great success. Using our pilot script and a preview of episodes to come, Hannah sold the package to networks on both sides of the Atlantic; with Richard Greene in the title role, *Robin Hood* ran for four years, generating profits for everyone concerned and perhaps, in some small way, setting the stage for the 1960s by subverting a whole new generation of young Americans. Meanwhile, Ian and I wrote two more pilots leading to network sales, *Sir Lancelot* and *The Buccaneers*, maintaining the demand not only for our own work but for that of a dozen other blacklistees whom we enlisted in our growing enterprise.

Everything was open between Hannah and us. But because the books of her company, Dilipa (named for her daughters, Dina, Lisa, and Paula), could be inspected by others, we received our payments under false names. We could open savings accounts under those names, we learned, since banks were less fussy about them than checking accounts. Then we would transfer the money to checking accounts in our real names. (Social Security regulations allow for aliases as long as you use your proper S.S. number.) Our record of three pilots written, three series sold to networks, was as good as any-body's in the business, and Hannah would have been happy to help us build new, pseudonymous reputations that might have helped us land jobs with U.S. networks and series producers. But the code of the blacklist made that impossible. While the same name could be used over and over again for banking purposes, our scriptwriting identities had to change constantly. Hannah's young story editor, Albert Ruben, was kept busy generating new names for us precisely in order to avoid the situation in which, seeing the same writer on more than one or two scripts, the network people in New York might ask to meet one of us as a prospect for other work.

From time to time, Hannah would invite us to London for face-to-face discussions. Ian, whose political acties had not resulted in a criminal prosecution or any special publicity, managed to secure a passport, and he made a couple of trips before moving his family to England in 1958. At first, I was not so lucky. The new head of the Passport Bureau, Frances Kilpatrick, deemed my travel abroad to be "not in the best interests of the United States." That same year, though, in the case of the artist Rockwell Kent, the Supreme Court ruled that no one could be denied a passport for political reasons. On hearing this news, I went to a photographer who advertised passport pictures and asked if I could have one immediately. It was the pre-Polaroid era, and he responded scornfully. If I really couldn't wait, I could use a coin-operated photo machine, he said. But if I did, he added gravely, "You'll end up looking like a Communist."

seven
Counter-Offensive

AT rare intervals, there appears among us a person whose virtues are so manifest to all, who has such a capacity for relating to every sort of human being, who so subordinates his own ego drive to the concerns of others, who lives his whole life in such harmony with the surrounding community that he is revered and loved by everyone with whom he comes in contact. Such a man Dalton Trumbo was not.

No one I've known can more aptly be described by the word "fascinating," but a word of almost opposite meaning, "abrasive," also belongs in the description. So, too, do a good many other modifiers, including wise, funny, greedy, generous, vain, biting, solicitous, ruthless, tender-hearted, devious, contentious, superbly rational, altruistic, prophetic, short-sighted, and indefatigable.

A determined indoorsman, Trumbo liked to write in the bathtub, pen in one hand, cigarette in the other. His major leisure activity was argument, carried on in voluminous correspondence with friends and strangers alike, and in conversations that, once Trumbo got going, made his listeners grow as forgetful of the hour as he was. It seems to me there are two general divisions of human temperament. One, comprising the vast majority and including many persons of superior talent and intelligence, embraces those who tend to accept the world as they find it, to go by the established rules and yield to the authority of expert opinion, particularly in fields outside the range of their special interests. The other kind, much fewer in number but large enough to contain its share of fools, scoundrels, geniuses, and mischief-makers, are inherently and often arrogantly skeptical, dismissing the solid credentials of expertise and insisting on proving each proposition by themselves, no matter how limited their qualifications for the task. Trumbo belonged unequivocally to the second group.

Late one night in our pre-blacklist days, I remember Trumbo walking me to my car outside his house on Beverly Drive, and waving his arms in a grand gesture that encompassed the neighbors for miles around. "All those crazy bastards sleeping away their eight hours," he said dismissively. "They're living only sixteen hours a day and I'm living twenty. So if I die when I'm sixty, and they live to be seventy, I'll still be ahead of them!"

Against all reasonable expectation, he made it to seventy, dying of lung cancer in 1976. But I think his figures were off anyway. He had lived at least three normal lives—a sheer outpouring of energy so disproportionate to the intake of fuel as to transcend the laws of physics. But with the possible exception of his astonishing antiwar novel, *Johnny Got His Gun*, I'd rate Trumbo's almost single-handed assault on the blacklist as the major achievement of his career.

As the blacklist solidified, Ian and I shifted our energies almost completely to writing for television, and our attitude was to make a living as best we could under the circumstances. Trumbo, by contrast, remained focused on the movies and, almost from the start, seemed to be looking for a way to bring the whole edifice of the blacklist tumbling down. In fact, when M.G.M. gave him his walking papers (shortly after Fox gave me mine), he refused to acknowledge the action, proceeding to finish the script he had been writing, turn it in, and request his next assignment (and paycheck). By these means and the lawsuit he filed when M.G.M. failed to deliver, he eventually extracted a small financial settlement.

After his move to Mexico, Trumbo wrote an original screen story and devised an elaborate cover to sell it in the Hollywood market. As part of a group of writers and journalists who had covered the Pacific theater in World War II, Trumbo had met a young New York newspaper man named Ray Murphy. Since Ray wanted to try his hand at screenwriting, Trumbo asked him to represent the script as his own and take it to a Hollywood agent to sell for him. In exchange, Ray was to keep one-third of the net proceeds up to a maximum of ten thousand dollars, and use the sale as a basis for his movie-writing career.

Ray followed instructions, and after some mixed reactions and a rewrite job, Trumbo heard that an agent was submitting the revised script around town. Then came silence. A month or more passed without word. Trumbo had grown concerned and impatient by the time he came across, in a three-week-old copy of the *Hollywood Reporter*, a story bearing the headline "20th Buys *Love Maniac*," that being the title of the work in question. He could only speculate and ruminate until, a few days later, Louella Parsons's column in the English-language *Mexico City News* reported the tragic death (from the flu) of young Ray Murphy, just after selling his first screen original. The amount of money involved was not revealed in the press, and Trumbo was still wondering how to approach Ray's family when a letter arrived from the dead man's brother, who had opened one from Trumbo and was seeking an explanation. Trumbo sent him a detailed account of the arrangement along with some letters from Ray to corroborate it, and a reasonable settlement of the affair ensued. His final net, of course, was only a fraction of what a Dalton Trumbo screenplay had brought in a few years earlier, but that was just a fact of blacklisted life.

Of all of us, Trumbo and our mutual friend Mike Wilson probably fared best in the black market while making the most trouble for the industry. Mike, though he had a quieter and less confrontational temperament than Trumbo, was a problem from the start, winning an Oscar in 1952 for the screenplay to *A Place in the Sun*, a job he had completed shortly before a H.U.A.C. appearance in which he took the Fifth. The response of the Producers Association was to declare all blacklistees ineligible for screen credit, even for old work that was belatedly released. As a result, *Friendly Persuasion* came out in 1956 with no credited screenwriter at all—a bizarre circumstance that threatened to wreak further havoc when the film won a Writer's Guild award and became an odds-on favorite for an Oscar, despite widespread awareness in Hollywood that the script was yet another Mike Wilson leftover.

To head off another major embarassment, the Academy passed a rule declaring that if a blacklistee's work (credited or otherwise) was nominated in any category, the nomination would be invalidated and the five nominees reduced to four. The Academy thus joined the three guilds in their full cooperation with the studio-enforced principle that not only jobs but credits could be denied on political grounds.

With the doors thus bolted, the leaders of the Academy approached the 1957 ceremonies confident that they would not again get caught honoring one of the miscreants. Among the Best Original story nominees that year, however, no one noticed the unknown "Robert Rich" in the credits of a low-budget sleeper, *The Brave One*, about a Mexican boy who raises a bull as a pet only to see him taken away for the bullfights. Announced as a winner, Rich's name failed to elicit any response until Jesse Lasky, Jr., a Screenwriters Guild vice president who had co-written *The Ten Commandments* the year before, stepped forward to accept the award on behalf of his "good friend" who, he reported, was at the bedside of his wife as she gave birth to their first child. Considering his total lack of preparation, Lasky handled his part well, not only repeating the producers' cover story with conviction but claiming the absent writer as an intimate. The following day, however, he had to admit that Robert Rich was neither a friend nor a member of the guild, nor, as far as anyone could tell, a real person—a separate one, that is, from Dalton Trumbo. For *The Brave One* was Trumbo's work, inspired by a trip to the bull ring in Mexico City, where he had learned about a rare pheomenon known as an *indulto*. When a bull has fought with unusual courage and grace, the crowd, if sufficiently moved by the animal's performance, may call on the matador to spare its life; this desire is expressed by a vigorous mass waving of handkerchiefs. Instinctively pro-bull, Trumbo had resisted Hugo Butler's invitations to the ring. One look at the spectacle of an *indulto*, however, and he saw the ingredients of a memorable movie climax.

The Brave One was one of several scripts that Trumbo wrote, under various names, for the King brothers, a trio of low-budget producers who were brutally honest about their eagerness to employ a writer they could not have afforded in ordinary times. Within the limits of their overstretched means, they treated him decently, even going as far as to help Trumbo finance the purchase of a house on his return to Los Angeles in early 1953. And they didn't seem to mind much when his cover got blown. Not that Trumbo himself ever acknowledged the rumors making him responsible for many of the best screenplays of the day, to the dismay of their actual authors. His coy position was that, under the circumstances, he could neither confirm nor deny authorship of any movie. But he could and did seize these opportunities to call attention to the growing black market and its injustices, and to introduce reporters to some of the other writers who had been forced to work under false names at cut rates.

A year after the Robert Rich affair, the Academy honored the script of *The Bridge on the River Kwai*. Once again, the recipient, Pierre Boule, failed to show up to collect his award; unlike Rich, Boule was a person in his own right—he was the author of the novel on which the movie had been based. He had never written a movie before, however, and, as would have been readily apparent if he had appeared on the podium, was a Frenchman with only a modest command of English, the language in which he had ostensibly written a screenplay notable for its elegance and its wit. Trumbo, who saw a comic side to the blacklist that tended to elude the rest of us, helpfully pointed out these facts to interested members of the press, who soon ascertained that *Kwai* was the work of Carl Foreman, a blacklisted writer-producer, and, once again, Mike Wilson, who was putting together perhaps the most distnguished record of any American screenwriter in the 1950s, blacklisted or otherwise.

The farce was not yet over. The next year, the Best Original Screenplay award went to the team of Nathan E. Douglas and Harold Jacob Smith for *The Defiant Ones*, the story of a white escaped convict (Tony Curtis) inconveniently shackled to a black one (Sidney Poitier). Douglas was, it turned out, a pseudonym for the blacklisted actor-turned-writer Nedrick Young. His writing partnership with the unblacklisted Smith proved to be nearly as problematic as the alliance between the two convicts in the movie. Weak-kneed as it was, the Academy could not bring itself to punish the innocent Smith for the sins of the guilty Young, so it reversed itself and reluctantly honored them both. It was getting harder and harder to keep us in our shadowy place.

The mood of the nation, meanwhile, was becoming more relaxed regarding applications of Cold War spirit to American nonconformists. In 1954, Senator McCarthy was censured by the Senate and the following years saw a reconstituted Supreme Court, under Chief Justice Earl Warren, reach a number of decisions that seemed to justify our 1947 stand, broadening its interpretation of the First Amendment and asserting that Congress could not function as a "law enforcement or trial agency" or expose for the sake of exposure.

In 1959, the Italian producer Carlo Ponti and his partner, Marcello Gerosi, summoned me to Hollywood to talk about rewriting a script for Ponti's wife, Sophia Loren, who was about to launch an American career at Paramount. Ponti, like other Europeans, found the blacklist mystifying, but the sponsorship of Paramount required him to observe the rituals. To maintain my cover, I was told to register in a hotel under a pseudonym so that the producers could speak to me through the Paramount switchboard without "violating security." I chose the first name Rick, so that if my own were used by mistake it might pass as a bit of carelessness, and the last name Spencer for no particular reason. When my daughter Ann, then a student at Stanford, came to visit me and share my quarters, a decent respect to the opinions of the day required that she should register as Miss Spencer rather than Miss Lardner.

The picture, *A Breath of Scandal*, ran into trouble while shooting in Vienna, the setting of the Ferenc Molnar play on which it was based. No one realized yet that the director, Michael Curtiz, who died the following year, was already a sick man. I was called in, did some more work on the script and returned to New York. Shooting was transferred to Rome to permit the reshooting of several love scenes by the famed Italian director Vittorio de Sica. I was summoned again by producers desperate to save what was becoming a lost cause of a movie. (Its other difficulties aside, Paramount had chosen, as Miss Loren's lover, a young actor named John Gavin who was not on the same plane in terms of either acting talent or inherent cinematic interest. Mr. Gavin would go on to serve as the United States Ambassador to Mexico in the Reagan years, and though I have no detailed knowledge of his work in that capacity, I am confident that it more than matched his performance in *A Breath of Scandal.* As for Miss Loren, it is a tribute to her abilities that a movie bad enough to kill some careers had virtually no effect on hers.)

It was in the Paramount office in Rome that I realized something I should have understood before about the nature of the blacklist. Paramount executives in Hollywood were increasingly concerned, and with good reason, about the poor footage that was coming into the lab. They wanted a key scene rewritten and reshot. A group of us sat around listening while the head of the Rome office conveyed our thinking to Y. Frank Freeman, the man who headed both the studio and the Motion Picture Producers Association. To my astonishment, I heard the speaker on our end repeatedly say that "Ring" thinks so-and-so or "Ring" feels such-and-such. Suddenly it became clear to me that Ponti and Gerosi could never have hired me without Freeman's permission. The need for a false name for the switchboard had never been a safeguard against the front office learning I was around but against someone at a much lower echelon leaking the information to one of the many anti-Communist vigilante groups that would have liked nothing better than to expose the studio's hypocrisy.

The blacklist had outlived its time, but it was not going to simply fade away. A force and a weapon were needed to strike the death blow. The force was Trumbo, and his principal weapon was ridicule.

When Kirk Douglas hired him to write the screenplay of *Spartacus*, Trumbo deliberately encouraged the British actors in the cast—Peter Ustinov, Laurence Olivier, and Charles Laughton—to come to his house to discuss their script problems with him. They had no sympathy for the strange American custom of making writers use pseudonyms, and with Trumbo's dispensation, they did what they could to circulate knowledge of his role on the picture.

From *Spartacus*, Trumbo proceeded to another Kirk Douglas project, the modern western *Lonely are the Brave*, and then to the Otto Preminger production of *Exodus*, a movie that was rushing toward production with all the elements in place except for a script. There was no script, that is, other than a 400-page opus that tried, like the Leon Uris novel on which it was based, to tell the entire story of the Jews from the Old Testament to the Twentieth Century. After reading the thousand-plus-page novel overnight, Trumbo convinced Otto that the movie should concentrate on the birth of Israel; then he worked through the Christmas and New Years holidays in order to meet the goal of delivering a workable screenplay by April 1960, when *Exodus* was scheduled to start shooting. With Douglas after him, simultaneously, for revisions on *Lonely Are the Brave*, Trumbo was overstretched even by his manic standards. Still, I think it was in this hectic period that, without ever exactly articulating it, he conceived the idea of setting his two employers against each other in a competition to see which of them would have the honor of breaking the blacklist and restoring him to his former standard of living.

In his days at Fox, Otto had bristled at the restraints of the studio system; the censorship code, in particular, was a constant annoyance to his middle-European sensibility. After previewing a rough cut of *Forever Amber*, he was summoned to New York for a conference with leaders of the Catholic Legion of Decency, where, to Otto's dismay, he saw Spyros Skouras, Zanuck's East Coast boss, knuckle under completely to the demands of a young enforcer in priest's garb. Otto would make any changes the legion required, Skouras promised. "Just show him what you want cut and he'll cut it." There ensued a day's worth of clerically monitored editing in which the movie (which, for all its dramatic shortcomings, had some risqué charm) lost, among other things, virtually every moment of contact between one character's lips and another's.

As a result of this and other unhappy experiences, Otto had negotiated the right to make a certain number of movies outside his arrangement with Fox, and by the mid-fifties he had left the studio orbit altogether, becoming an independent producer—one with, by the terms of the agreement he demanded and got from United Artists, complete control over the editing of his films. Flexing his muscles, he fought the censors repeatedly while making some of the boldest movies of the decade, including *The Man with a Golden Arm*, *Anatomy of a Murder*, *Carmen Jones*, and *The Moon Is Blue*. In the case of the last-named picture, he ignored the protests of both the Hays office and the Legion of Decency, refusing to cut a line, and with a movie officially and loudly denounced by the church hierarchy, made the invigorating discovery that most American Catholics (to say nothing of non-Catholics) seemed to look elsewhere for their moviegoing guidance. The experience also taught Otto that by defending a mild comedy from attacks, he could generate the kind of publicity and controversy that no amount of advertising money could have bought.

Grateful to Trumbo for salvaging *Exodus*, Otto informed his United Artists backers that he had decided to make the writer's identity official. He explained later (and I have no doubt truthfully) that he considered it "absolutely a crime" the way, having served our sentences, we were being denied our livelihoods or employed at rates of pay far below what we would have commanded in an open market. It is probably also relevant to note, however, that Trumbo's work on *Spartacus* was now an open secret, inevitably raising in Otto's mind the possibility that, if *he* didn't take the plunge, he might be remembered for tolerating an injustice that someone else then decided to repudiate. Douglas was, in fact, also close to Trumbo, who had now written a couple of his best roles. He didn't have Otto's chutzpah, however, or his comfort level with defiance, and he doubted that he could sell Universal, the studio behind *Spartacus*, on the idea of giving Trumbo credit. So it was that, on January 19, 1961, I bought an early edition of the *New York Times* with a front-page story revealing Trumbo as the screenwriter of *Exodus*—a piece of news that spread quickly through the extended blacklist diaspora in Los Angeles, Mexico, New York, and France, signaling us that the end was near.

But not quite at hand, even though Douglas and Universal, prodded by Otto's action, soon followed suit and both epics were box-office hits. (They faced picket lines in a few cities, organized by the American Legion and the Catholic War Veterans, but, as Otto had anticipated, few potential ticket-buyers paid much heed.) The blacklist had never been officially acknowledged, and thus couldn't easily be disowned. For the better part of another decade, the question of employment and credit had to be fought out producer by producer, studio by studio, and writer by writer.

Shortly after the *Exodus* story broke, Frank Sinatra announced the hiring of the blacklisted writer Albert Maltz to write a movie about Eddie Slovik, the only American soldier executed for desertion in World War II. Like Preminger, Sinatra was denounced; unlike him, Sinatra caved in, paying off Maltz in cash and eventually scrubbing the project, perhaps partly out of fear of harming his friend John F. Kennedy, a candidate for President at the time. (Following the election that fall, however, the President-elect and his brother, Attorney-

General-to-be Robert Kennedy, crossed a picket line to see *Spartacus* at a theater in Washington D.C., and pronounced it good.) Another six years passed before Albert got his name on the screen with *Two Mules for Sister Sara*.

In 1961, American audiences saw a version of *Lawrence of Arabia* that listed the playwright Robert Bolt as sole screenwriter, though Mike Wilson (who had done the first draft) got joint credit everywhere else. Lester Cole, my fellow Danbury alumnus, had to settle for a pseudonymous credit on "Born Free" as late as 1965; Columbia Pictures had tried to remove him from the project altogether, but its formerly blacklisted producer, Carl Foreman, had refused. Abe Polonsky's career as a director suffered a twenty-year gap between *Force of Evil*, in 1948, and *Tell Them Willie Boy Is Here*, in 1968. And, of course, many more blacklistees never made it back at all. Only about ten percent of us, in fact, managed to go back into the movies, according to Larry Ceplair and Steven Englund's book "The Inquisition in Hollywood."

In my case, another two years of semi-surreptitious work intervened before I could write under my own name. It was Otto, once again, who made that possible, by announcing in 1962 that he had hired me to adapt a book called *Genius* by Patrick Dennis. The American Legion responded with a letter of protest, demanding to know why he couldn't find a "patriotic writer" for the job. Just as it was their right to boycott the movie when it was released, Otto replied, so was it his right to pick a screenwriter.

Genius was never made. Otto had said from the start that the movie required a top star, and none of those he pursued—Laurence Olivier, Rex Harrison, and Alec Guiness—proved to be available. True to form, however, Otto had me working sub rosa on *The Cardinal*, the movie he was shooting while *Genius* was in the works. That fall, I accompanied him to Vienna and then to Rome, ostensibly to confer about *Genius*, but in reality so I could edit what he was going to film the next day. In Rome I discovered that he also had Gore Vidal writing parts of the picture, which ended up, remarkably enough, as quite a respectful view of the Roman Catholic Church, for all the grief that some of its representatives had given him over the years. I don't know whether Otto realized that both Gore and I were atheists. Another thing we had in common, and which we jointly communicated to him, was our verdict that he had fallen into the habit of buying the movie rights to some of the worst-written best-sellers on the market.

With my future as a screenwriter still difficult to assess, I responded eagerly to an invitation to collaborate with Ian on a musical. We would be doing the book and Ian's old friend Johnny Mercer, with whom he had written *Second Chorus* twenty years earlier, the lyrics. (It was Johnny's one great professional frustration that, for all his triumphs as a songwriter and performer, he had never been part of a successful Broadway show.) The production, an adaptation of Ben Jonson's *Volpone* relocated to the Yukon in the time of the 1898 gold rush, had been conceived for a commemorative festival in Dawson City, where it was the reopening attraction of a historic opera house in the summer of 1963. With Bert Lahr as a vengeful prospector and Larry Blyden as his slippery sidekick, *Foxy* rewarded us with not only the satisfaction of operating in a new medium and finding we could make it work, but with the joy of watching top professional performers take our material and build on it. Back in New York, the producer, Robert Whitehead, was preparing to mount the show on Broadway the following season when he was offered the job of running, with Elia Kazan, the theater company of the nascent Lincoln Center for the Performing Arts. We liked and trusted Whitehead and lamented his loss, but from a commercial standpoint our show didn't seem to have suffered much since David Merrick, perhaps the most successful Broadway producer of the postwar era, swiftly stepped into the breach.

Mercer and I, in fact, were so optimistic that we broke the old rule against creative people putting up their own money. My share, I remember, was thirty thousand dollars; Johnny's must have been substantially more than that. And our bet was still looking good when *Foxy* began its pre-Broadway tryout in Cleveland, generating enthusiastic reviews, large audiences, and plentiful laughter. Standing in the back of the theater taking all this in, none of us paid much attention to a development unfolding in New York that, in hindsight, was fatal to our efforts. I am referring to the highly successful opening of another Merrick production, *Hello Dolly*.

In our naïveté, we had failed to take note of an important nuance in the business arrangements. By the time Merrick agreed to produce our show, it was already fully financed. That meant that neither Merrick himself, nor any of his regular backers, had a stake in it. As soon as theatergoers began lining up for *Dolly*, he made it plain with his every *Foxy*-related deed that the promotion of that other production and the maximization of its profits had become his consuming interest, without regard for the effects on what he had sized up as our less financially promising enterprise. In that spirit, Merrick didn't even bother to exercise a contract requiring RCA Victor to record an original cast album—standard procedure for any musical that survived its opening. Instead, he encouraged RCA to defer the *Foxy* album and spend the money it had thereby saved marketing the *Dolly* album.

We were dealing, by now, not just with one of Broadway's great showmen, but with two, for on opening night, amid the post-performance celebrating, Merrick sold the production to Billy Rose, owner of the Ziegfeld Theater, where *Foxy* was in residence. The reviews were favorable if not ecstatic, and perhaps that fact had a tempering effect on Rose's enthusiasm; like Merrick, however, his attention soon seemed to shift elsewhere—in his case, not to another show but to a former wife whom he chose, at this moment, to remarry and with whom he abruptly departed on a second honeymoon before even signing the papers sealing his handshake deal with Merrick. Thus we found ourselves without anyone who could properly be called a producer, and without a line of advertising or promotion of any sort.

Still, with all four authors waiving the royalties due us, and with neither impresario doing a thing on its behalf, *Foxy* ran for nine weeks in the cavernous Ziegfeld. Its closing was a grave disappointment to all of us, the more so to Johnny and me because of our investments. Four decades later, however, I can still relish the memory of Bert Lahr impersonating a British aristocrat and singing this Mercer lyric:

> Dear were the homes of Cheltenham
> Large were the hearts that dwelt in 'em
> I but a tad of a lad
> Mum and Dad at the pub—just beltin' 'em away
> Now I've attained seniority
> And come to my majority
> I've travelled far
> Tasted snails—caviar
> So with some authority—I say
>
> If you want a bon vivant to brighten up the scene
> Or a jolly extra man to give the party sheen
> Strolling on the Parthenon—or bowling on the green
> I play mandolin—and tambourine
> Will travel . . .

As it turned out, I had entered a period of working for fickle producers. Shortly after *Foxy's* demise, Martin Ransohoff, an independent moviemaker with a good deal of street smarts and not as much polish, hired me to adapt a novel about a poker-playing showdown between a young card shark played by Steve McQueen and an old pro played, or so we expected, by Spencer Tracy. In the summer of 1964, *The Cincinnati Kid* took me back to Hollywood and into the gates of the much-diminished Metro-Goldwyn-Mayer, which was financing the production. Louis B. Mayer was, of course, long gone, and his great studio was contracting fast. For a brief moment, however, it looked as if we had a chance of claiming, as a dividend for casting Tracy, a cameo appearance by Kate Hepburn as the Tracy character's old flame.

Tracy, however, was not in the best of health and was playing hard to get. Soon after my arrival, accordingly, Ransohoff asked me to join him in a visit to Tracy's cottage off Sunset Boulevard, with the object of overcoming our intended star's resistance. For me, it was a first chance to see the two since *Woman of the Year* twenty-three years earlier. It was also an opportunity to thank Kate for her letter to the parole board, which (embarrassed by such expressions of gratitude) she chose to deny having sent. Both Kate and Spencer were generous, on the other hand, in their praise of the automobile that Mike Kanin and I had given them; they had used it, they told me, to tow a succession of broken-down vehicles of more recent vintage into the shop.

For reasons that may have been more apparent to Randoshoff than they were to me, he elected to make small talk about a movie biography of another former M.G.M. star, Jean Harlow. "And guess who they're casting as Harlow?" he exclaimed, naming a popular actress of the sixties whom he described, with evident disgust, as "the titless wonder." It was not in Marty's nature to consider the indelicacy of such a comment in front of Hepburn, whose beauty had never been the buxom kind. My eyes went to Tracy as his did to her, to gauge her reaction. Whatever it was, she didn't reveal it.

Had there been any real prospect of wooing either of them into our movie, I'm not convinced that Ransohoff's brand of salesmanship would have been up to the task. Even before our visit, however, M.G.M. had effectively vetoed Tracy, who was accustomed to getting $400,000 a picture, in favor of Edward G. Robinson, who could be had for a quarter of that amount (and who nevertheless gave a fine performance in the movie, as did Steve McQueen and Tuesday Weld).

Hollywood had changed profoundly over the years of my exile, and in some ways for the better, to judge by my initial experience with *The Cincinnati Kid*. Sam Peckinpah, our director, held a reading of the script with the actors and me sitting around a table, and when one of them raised an objection to a line or an action, I was in a position to adjust it. When shooting began, I returned to New York confident that for once a picture would come out more or less as I had written it. In a matter of days, however, I learned that Ransohoff had fired Peckinpah, ostensibly for shooting an unauthorized nude scene featuring the actress Sharon Tate. As if this was not disconcerting enough, his designated replacement, Norman Jewison, was bringing in a new writer, Terry Southern. His reason for doing so was evidently not any profound objection to my script; many of the changes they made were cosmetic, including a shift of locale from St. Louis to the more picturesque New Orleans, where they could incorporate one of the famous funeral parades that take place in that city.

My next movie assignment was another lesson—a more satisfying one—in the ways of the new Hollywood. It began when I received the galleys of a comic novel about an army medical unit in the Korean War, written by a surgeon who had served in such a unit and a professional writer recruited by the publisher, William Morrow. What Morrow wanted from me, and I happily supplied, was a book-jacket blurb. ("Not since *Catch 22* has the struggle to maintain sanity in the rampant insanity of war been told in such outrageously funny terms.") Then I found myself wondering whether the novel, with its ramshackle structure and mordant humor, could be made into a movie. Not easily. Robert Altman, who read it only after he had signed on to direct my screenplay, commented that he would never have considered the book as film material. For one thing, a major plot point was that in order to raise money to send their Korean houseboy to college in Maine, the doctors made one of the medics up to look like Jesus Christ on the cross. Then they took him on a tour of army posts where they introduced him as the Savior and sold photographs of him autographed with the Holy Name. Even in the post-studio Hollywood of 1970, this was not going to pass muster. Nor would a scene in which the dentist, known as the Painless Pole, took what his buddies assured him was a suicide pill after losing his sexual prowess. His unit then arranged to have him dropped unconscious from a helicopter with an open parachute, and on recovering he found tied to his all-star penis a blue ribbon, which somehow restored his male ego. I had to invent a character called Lieutenant Dish, worried about returning to her husband in a state of sexual frustration, and have the hero, Hawkeye, let her glimpse the dentist's naked body and proceed to take care of Painless's problem and her own.

And, of course, all through the movie version, I was looking for ways to deal with story developments in visual rather than narrative terms. In the book, for instance, when Hawkeye realizes he has seen a new co-worker before but can't remember where or when, the answer comes to him undramatically after days of frustration. In the movie, Trapper John intercepts a football and throws his "Dartmouth pass" right into Hawkeye's arms, triggering his memory.

After reading the novel, I passed it on to Ingo Preminger, who had been my agent throughout the blacklist days and since. Ingo was, like me, eager to play a less reactive role in the movie business, and he quickly read *M*A*S*H* and agreed not only to sell the project but to produce it himself. Meanwhile, though, I had developed misgivings that led me to give the book to Ian. After he had read it, I told him what I was worried about. It wasn't really a novel, I had decided, but a series of short stories about the same characters in the same place and time. And the comedy depended on their maintaining the same iconoclastic attitude from beginning to end. I was struggling with a basic rule of dramaturgy: One of the things that makes a good story, I had always believed, was a character or characters changing in the course of it. In this case, in violation of the rule, the two heroes, Hawkeye and Trapper John, would be exactly the same people at the end as at the beginning.

Ian saw the point and responded to it cogently. "Forget the rule," he told me, and I did.

Before long, Ingo had made a deal with the studio that had summarily dismissed me in 1947. Indeed, Fox was now under the active management of Darryl Zanuck's son Richard and his partner David Brown, and the elder Zanuck, though he had moved into a sort of semi-retirement in Paris, was officially back as president of the company. In all our *M*A*S*H* experience, however, I don't remember a word of recrimination or regret passing anyone's lips, or, indeed, any reference at all to my prior association with the studio. The blacklist, we all now seemed to agree, had been one of those acts of nature for which it would be petty and small-minded to assign any personal responsibility.

Richard Zanuck, Brown, Ingo, and I were very enthusiastic about *M*A*S*H*. At first, not too many other people were. More than a dozen directors turned it down before Ingo sold the rest of us on the

almost unknown Altman, whose accomplishments at the time consisted of a large body of television work and a couple of little-noticed
feature films. We were a mature team by Hollywood's evolving standards, Bob in his mid-forties, Ingo and I our mid-fifties, and grand-
fathers the lot of us. It was a source of satisfaction to me, at any rate,
that this trio of comparative graybeards could jointly create a film
that proved to be immensely popular with the younger moviegoers
Hollywood had been losing in the fifties and sixties. (When Ingo
made this point to reporters, however, Altman bristled, not wanting
to be lumped with us geezers.) I was also pleased by the realization
that, through our comic tale of a war that the nation had begun to forget, we could illuminate something about the military mindset and
cultural arrogance of the war that was on every American's mind—
the one we were waging in Vietnam.

For about two minutes, Ingo and I weighed the idea of transferring
M*A*S*H from Korea to Vietnam. But the current war was just too
close for us to be funny or properly irreverent about it. By keeping
our story at a safe distance in years and miles, we could safely look
askance at an America military adventure in Asia, and let people
draw their own parallels.

Bob Altman made a number of major contributions to the finished
product. One, building on a single scene in the script where "Hot
Lips" Houlihan's lovemaking with Frank Burns was broadcast to the
entire encampment, was to make the P.A. system a recurring element
throughout the movie. He also added the business of the stolen Jeep
at the beginning and the subplot of an affair between the nurse
Leslie and Colonel Blake, and he was responsible for several notable
pieces of dialogue, including what is probably the movie's biggest
laugh: Dago Red saying, "He was drafted," in answer to Hot Lips'
furious rhetorical question about how someone like Hawkeye ever
got into a position of such responsibility. (Part of the reason the line

got such a big laugh, though, was that for once Bob stopped all the extraneous noise, allowing the words to be heard clearly. A number of what I thought were pretty funny lines when I wrote them had to compete with a high volume of incidental chatter going on at the same time.)

He made a few miscalls as well. That was my assessment, at any rate, of some extreme slapstick in the opening scene and of a later bit in which, for no apparent reason, virtually the entire company joined Hawkeye and Duke in singing "Onward Christian Soldiers" in response to the spectacle of Major Burns on his knees, praying. And Bob let the football game drag on to a length far beyond its proper proportion in the story. But these were minor failings alongside all the good things that he added, including the powerful glimpses of combat surgery, which made the extracurricular antics of the heroes much easier to understand. At the end of the screening where I first saw those sequences, however, one of the other members of the small audience registered his strong disapproval. This was Darryl Zanuck, who, after watching *M*A*S*H* with a very young French actress friend of his, summoned the key people involved to the back of the projection room in order to tell us that the whole thing was an outrageous breach of taste. "You simply can't combine broad comedy and bloody operating-room scenes," he declared, with all the weight of his long experience as an arbiter of the acceptable and unacceptable. There would be a meeting in his office at ten o'clock the next morning, it was decreed, to decide on the re-cutting and re-shooting that would be needed to make the movie fit for release.

At the appointed hour, however, Zanuck announced that no changes would be necessary after all. "Turned out my friend liked those operating room scenes," he told us. "So maybe the young people will go for the picture." It was the first time anyone could remember the old man's lechery leading to a constructive result.

eight

"Humoring you cost us twenty thousand dollars."

TWO Oscars, one for best original screenplay, the other for best screenplay adapted from another medium; the Writers Guild West's Laurel Award for distinguished achievement; a similar award (named for my friend Ian Hunter) from the Writers Guild East; the 1998 Nantucket Film Festival's First Annual Writer's Tribute—it sounds like a pretty impressive movie career. In fact, I'm impressed myself when I hear my accomplishments recited on a podium. What isn't mentioned—what my admirers don't even know about actually—are the unproduced scripts, just about twice as many on the shelf as ever made it to the screen. About twenty times in sixty years, I have typed a title page and the introductory "FADE IN:" with the expectation that the hundred or hundred and fifty

pages I proceeded to write would be converted into the film I visu-
alized, and . . . it didn't happen.

Add in the occasions when a script gets "rewritten" at the behest of
a director or producer (to say nothing of the alterations made by actors,
cutters, or—the final affront—those unknown apparatchiks engaged
in what is euphemistically called editing for television), and you can
begin to see why I have never been much of an evangelist for my chosen profession. A publisher, magazine editor, or theatrical producer
may all make suggestions, but it is the writer who does the rewrite or
looks for another sponsor. For the screenwriter, ninety-nine percent of
the time, there is no control over the transition from concept to frames
of exposed film, and once the transition has been made, no previous
version retains any significant reality. How can I match my paper draft
of a scene against what is now implanted on celluloid?

In the spring of 1980, I got a phone call from Ray Stark, one of
Hollywood's most successful and powerful executives, who wanted me
to consider working on a new version of *Pal Joey*, with Al Pacino as
the star and Herbert Ross as the director. I would be free, he assured
me, to start afresh with the original John O'Hara stories, and we would
have access not only to the superb score of the original show but also
to any other Rodgers and Hart number that suited our needs. Ross, a
director I admired, was having a lot of commercial success at the time,
and after a series of meetings, I laid out some ideas to which he
responded with such enthusiasm that I agreed to do the script. Stark,
in an equally effusive manner, promised to work out a deal with my
agent while Frances and I went off on a ten-day vacation in Italy.

When my agent contacted Stark's office after my return, he was told
they needed a week to clear up a "technicality" concerning the rights
to the material. And that was the last we ever heard from either Stark
or Ross about the matter. What became of the updated *Pal Joey*? I can't
tell you because I don't have a clue myself. It was just another stage in

my endless education on the subject of producer-writer relations, which began when I was twenty-two and turned in the first screenplay I had written without a collaborator. I couldn't wait for the producer's reaction, but I wasn't expecting to hear it before he had opened the script. "I'm sending this right over to Wald and Macaulay," he said, referring to a well-paid writing team on the Warner lot. "I gave it to you so you could break ground for them while they were finishing another job." It was hard to believe he was going to pass it on without reading a word, but that is just what he did. And on what basis could I object? I had been paid for my work, almost a thousand dollars as I remember it.

In terms of control, it was the fact of, rather than the amount of, payment that counted. When Mike Kanin and I sold *Woman of the Year*, we received a record sum, but in a transmutation so prodigious it could only be achieved by contract, Metro-Goldwyn-Mayer became the "author" of the work. If anyone remains skeptical about this process, let him take note that when a Broadway musical version of that 1942 movie was produced forty years later, authors' royalties for the source material went to M.G.M.

I recall the only time I thought, temporarily, that I had won an argument with Darryl Zanuck. We were discussing quite seriously (all such discussions seem of transcendent importance at the time) his proposal to cut from the script of *Forever Amber* a scene I thought essential to understanding the motivation of the leading character. Although motivation scenes were a prime Zanuck target (he preferred to strip any film down to pure action), he finally conceded that I might, in this case, have a point, and instructed Otto Preminger, the producer-director, to shoot the scene. A couple of months later we sat in a projection room, watching a rough assemblage of the movie, and the scene in question, which I never did see on film, was gone. Zanuck directed a comment at me over his shoulder: "Humoring you on that one cost us twenty thousand dollars."

That closed the subject for good, and properly so. If I had pointed out that I still found the character's motivation unclear, I would have been ignoring the several facts incorporated in his one short statement. It was a fact that I had wanted to retain the scene; it was a fact that he had made the binding decision to eliminate it; therefore, it was equally true that I had made a mistake costing the studio something like twenty thousand dollars.

The decision to put a new writer on a project caused Irving Thalberg or David Selznick no more angst than a football coach feels about sending in a wide receiver to announce the next play. But at least if yours happened to be the final script approved by the man in charge, you knew no one else had the authority to make changes from then on. By the mid-forties, the pioneering generation of studio bosses was beginning to pass from the scene and one of our beclouded visions of the postwar world was the idea that, in the less hierarchical and factory-like movie business to come, writers would have more opportunity to choose their projects and find collaborators and financing for them. Little did we suspect that, quite apart from the blacklist, the future would bring a *reduction* rather than an increase in the writer's status.

My first experience with the new ethos came when Ian Hunter and I, under a pseudonym, wrote a screenplay for a British company. After meeting with the producers and the director on the Caribbean island where the movie was to be filmed, we made some necessary changes. Then, just before shooting began, we were startled to receive a "final shooting script" that was quite a drastic rewrite of ours, with the added defect of being, in our opinion, not nearly as good. Sidney Poitier told me later that he and John Cassavetes, who had agreed to do the picture, *Virgin Island*, based on our script, shared our disappointment in the new one. The producers' only response to our protest was that standard British practice entitled the director to a final revision after the writers were through. (Our pseudonym, Philip Rush, remained intact on the screen credits, and when the movie was released in London, a historian of that name wrote an indignant letter to the *Times*, disclaiming responsibility.)

By the time I was able to write under my own name again, this inflation of the director's authority was already taking hold in Hollywood, as my experience on the *Cincinnati Kid* taught me. Soon it had reached a point where, as a condition of agreeing to do a movie, a director could single-handedly change its whole purpose and thrust, even though no other party to the production had seen the need for such an adjustment.

I had done a couple of drafts of an adaptation of *Semi-Tough*, a book about professional football by Dan Jenkins. The producer liked it; Jenkins liked it; most important of all, according to the old standards, the heads of United Artists liked it enough to take the crucial step from "developing the property" to scheduling it for production as a starring vehicle for Burt Reynolds. The only missing element was a director, who was suddenly supplied in the person of Michael Ritchie. Although I conveyed to him indirectly my willingness to discuss even major revisions of the script, he told the studio he didn't want to talk to the old writer; he wanted to talk to a new writer. He also announced that he wanted to make *Semi-Tough* a satirical comedy not about professional football but about consciousness-raising groups.

The producer and the studio regarded these demands as arbitrary but not excessive. They displayed their adaptability by transferring their entrepreneurial endorsement from the book and screenplay they had bought and set for production to whatever Ritchie and his new writer might devise to take their place. (The new writer was a friend and one of the best in the business, Walter Bernstein, who called me when he was offered the job and received my blessing, just as I would have received his if the situation had been reversed.)

Some of the leading directors when I first went to Hollywood—
Howard Hawks and William Wyler for example—viewed themselves
more like directors in the theater interpreting what the writer had
conceived, though of course they had far more to do than a stage
director. The idea of the director as a creative force took root in
Europe after World War II when figures like Federico Fellini and
Francois Truffaut actually thought up their own ideas for their films
and used writers sparingly, if at all. Except for Billy Wilder, John
Huston, and a few other cases, that didn't happen in American
movies until quite recently. But the idea of the all-powerful director
is so much a part of the job description now that even among members of the profession who make no pretense of being writers and are
in no danger of being compared to Billy Wilder or John Huston, total
authority has become the norm—and bringing in a new writer is just
one of the standard ways of asserting it.

Under the circumstances, you're lucky to wind up, as I did in the
case of *M*A*S*H*, with a director whose abilities aren't drastically
outstripped by his ego, who sees the material as you do, and who
makes changes that more often than not are improvements. But if the
movie is a hit, it's best not to expect anyone to think you had very
much to do with it.

The first hint of *M*A*S*H*'s extraordinary success came at the
Cannes Film Festival, where it won the Grand Prix. My own presence at the festival was something of a fluke, precipitated by a conversation over supper with the Preminger brothers. "Ring, are you
going to Cannes?" Otto inquired.

"Hell no," I said, "nobody ever invites a writer to go."

"Ingo, how come?" Otto said, disapprovingly. "I'm taking *my* writer."

Thus was Ingo inspired to ask Fox to pay my travel expenses,
arguing that my presence, as one of the Hollywood Ten, would make
a useful publicity angle.

When I got to Cannes and began to sense the interest that our movie was generating, I thought it prudent to jot down some ideas to discuss with some of the horde of reporters in attendance. There had been talk about whether *M*A*S*H* was an "antiwar movie." That struck me as a diversion; if there were any pro-war people around, a movie wasn't going to change their minds. But the picture did have an incidental comment to make about a special kind of war, one waged in a weak country, far away, by a strong country—or, more particularly, an American war on the Asian mainland.

Some people had portrayed *M*A*S*H* as an attack on religion, and I thought I had better address that issue as well. It wasn't about religion per se, I reasoned, just about the inappropriateness of religious sentiment in the combat zone. War is such a distinctly man-made institution, it seems to me, that it is quite unfair to involve God in it at all.

I had prepared these thoughts, for a press conference, and sure enough there was one, following a screening of the film on the second morning after our arrival. But I didn't make any of my points because I wasn't there. Whoever was supposed to tell me about it hadn't, and, as far as I know, my absence didn't provoke any outcry from the assembled masses.

It would be misleading to leave the impression that no interest whatsoever was expressed in my contribution to the picture during my whole two weeks in Europe. In Hamburg a few days before we got to Cannes, a commentator from an intellectual weekly said he knew I had been imprisoned and blacklisted as one of the "Hollywood Ten." Was this obnoxious, reactionary, and militaristic film, he wanted to know, the price I had had to pay in order to work under my own name again? Otherwise, everyone seemed to assume that the director (who had not even been part of the project until I had written two drafts of the script) had created the movie pretty much unassisted and that he alone was capable of explaining what it meant.

Bob himself, understandably, was rather charmed by the idea that *M*A*S*H* had sprung pretty much full-blown from his head. He suggested in several interviews that he had treated the script as a mere blueprint, and, I regret to say that, for my own part, I failed to give him his rightful, and large, degree of credit the following spring when I accepted my Academy Award. I can only say in my defense that I fully expected Bob to be up there on the podium later in the evening to accept the Best Director award that went instead to Franklin Schaffner for *Patton*.

Bob had encouraged the actors in *M*A*S*H* to improvise many of their lines. Maybe that's what he had in mind when he implied that he had all but discarded the screenplay. (The only time I visited the set during shooting, he made a joke of it, calling out, "Hey, somebody find the script! Here comes the writer!") But the departures weren't as drastic as he made out; much of the improvisation involved a couple of scenes between Donald Sutherland and Elliot Gould in which they rephrased lines in their own words. Even in those scenes, they stuck to the basic outlines of what I had written, and as any screenwriter will tell you, dialogue is not the essence of a movie script.

When silent movies became the "talkies," Hollywood studios imported Broadway's most successful playwrights to fill the new need for dialogue. Both parties saw little difference between a drama performed by live actors in a theater and one recorded by the new sound cameras, and both were dismayed when audiences found many early talkies wordy and tedious. The devices the movie-makers had developed in the silent days—the close-up, the reverse angle, the moving shot, the abrupt cut, the dissolve, the divided screen, different lenses, varying depth of focus, montage, camera speeds, flashbacks and flash forwards among other novel techniques—had created a whole new storytelling language. For the first time, that language included sound, which meant sound effects and background music as well as dialogue. But the spoken word turned out not to have the same all-important significance it had on the stage. You couldn't plant a vital story point in a line of dialogue and be sure it had registered; you had to reinforce it with another plant, preferably a visual one.

Waldo Salt has described our craft as "a separate form, and what it is, is writing in images. There is a separate aesthetic that is quite different from the theater or the novel. It comes closer to the technique of poetry." Waldo was a talented amateur artist, and the rough pages of his movie scripts were full of sketches of the action as he envisioned it. I happen to be completely inept at drawing, but when I am writing a movie, my attention goes back and forth between the word processor and an imaginary screen on which the action I'm conceiving is taking place. The sight—what is included in the shot and what is not—and the sound, if any, are equally important, and are complementary in the sense that each serves to limit the need for the other.

Half the strength of a successful movie, Irving Thalberg once said, lies in its basic idea, whether it comes from a book, a play, or an original screenplay. It is important, however, to understand what constitutes a movie idea. Many would-be writers think that a subject ("Let's make a movie about the Bayou country in Louisiana," or "Nobody's made a picture about a tyrannical captain in the 18th-century British Navy") is the same thing as an idea. A character or background that hasn't been dealt with before can be a valuable asset, but it's still a long way from an idea for a movie. Even if you say a tyrannical captain and a law-abiding first mate, you're not there yet. You still have to develop it: "The situation becomes so intolerable that the first mate, despite his loyal adherence to form and tradition, leads a mutiny against the captain." Then you have a dramatic situation that will work not only for this movie but against other backgrounds as well. Thus, when a friend of mine saw *Red*

River and congratulated its screenwriter, Borden Chase, his reaction was, "You didn't get it? It's *Mutiny on the Bounty.*"

With *M*A*S*H*, the idea originated neither with Bob Altman nor with me but with the co-authors of the book. For all of Bob's interpolations and improvisations, however, the basic structure of the movie is the one laid out in my script, and each scene has the beginning, middle, and end that I gave it.

The last movie that I wrote, *The Greatest*, was the life story of Muhammad Ali, with Ali himself in the role. The director, Tom Gries, and I worked closely together, and when shooting was over, he explained to me just how he planned to assemble the footage, which had been shot in a somewhat haphazard fashion. Taking a couple of days off to relax before he went into the editing room, Tom was playing a vigorous game of tennis when he suffered a heart attack and died on the court. After the shock wore off, I realized what a problem it was going to be for strangers to edit the picture in anything like the way Tom had devised in his head. So I instructed my agent Jim Preminger (Ingo's son), to ask the studio, Columbia Pictures, to let the assistant director and me serve as an advisory committee to the film editor in order to convey as much as we could of Tom's intentions. I offered to join the effort without any compensation. Columbia promptly rejected the offer, establishing instead an advisory committee composed of studio executives who, they said, would know better what would work at the box office. The movie they came up with, besides departing in a number of ways from Tom's plan and my screenplay, didn't work particularly well at the box office either.

It is a temptation for a writer to fantasize that his unshot scripts could have become more original and provocative movies than the ones that ran the gauntlet to theatrical exhibition. A sober review of the files in my case shows that this would be self-delusion. Among the unproduced screenplays are a sizable number that were poor ideas to begin with, undertaken for misguided or unworthy motives, including the classic cop-out of the indentured artist: "If they're dumb enough to pay all that money for this crap, who am I to object?" In the end, "my best scripts are on the shelf" has to be amended to "my best and worst." But there still remain just enough of the former to make up a small but rewarding festival of superior pictures. The greatest appeal of this imaginary festival is the brilliant fidelity with which my scripts have been translated into film. In what other festival has each entry been photographed with flawless taste, accented with an unassuming yet telling musical score, directed with imaginative respect and played to the hilt but not an inch beyond by inspired and selfless actors?

My festival of unrealized films begins with my first original story, which was definitely ahead of its time. Five years before Charles Brackett and Billy Wilder wrote *The Lost Weekend*, I had outlined a movie about a woman ravaged by alcoholism. The part is still played by Carole Lombard in my imagination, because it was Carole who responded with such excitement and took my story from studio to studio, only to be told by all of them that the subject was unacceptable.

Early in World War II, I read a short story in a magazine by Ira Wolfert, who had covered the fall of France as a war correspondent. There were so few available young men for the French resistance that they had to recruit elderly ones to take the rap when the Nazis closed in on them. The dramatic conflict arose from the fact that one of these recruits was a lifelong bum who made no distinction between the conquerors and the French police he had always defied. All that interested him was the food and shelter offered for signing up to be a potential martyr. I sold Dalton Trumbo on the idea, and together we wrote a screenplay, *The Fishermen of Beaudrais*. No studio offered us what we considered a reasonable price and the project was never sold, though the script was admired at the time and again, more than half a century later, when it was chosen for publication in an issue of *Scenario* magazine.

In 1946, just after the war, Trumbo and I were part of a group of six or seven writers and one producer who decided that the best way to fight the studio system was to choose our ideas, write the scripts, and only then try to get a studio to back us as a production unit. We began by optioning the film rights to a wonderful novel, Christina Stead's *The Man Who Loved Children*. Most of my partners in the new company had existing commitments. I didn't, and happily undertook the task of converting the book into a screenplay. The beauty of the story lies in the title character, who loves only himself but devotes all his time to his children because they alone are tolerant enough to listen to him recount his virtues and accomplishments. When I had done a draft and revised it in accordance with my partners' criticisms, we were ready to look for financial backing. At that moment, history intervened in the form of the Un-American Activities Committee and its subpoenas. Our independent artists' company was stillborn, and *The Man Who Loved Children* was relegated to my private festival. (Other filmmakers, including John Huston, later glimpsed the rich movie possibilities in that book, but it remains unproduced.)

After the enormous success of *M*A*S*H*, I had plenty of job offers; that, in turn, led me to choose the boldest and most controversial subjects—and the ones most likely to be rejected by a nervous front office. In the early seventies, I read a novel called *Farragan's Retreat*, a black comedy about a Roman Catholic family in Philadelphia so disgraced when one of its scions flees to Montreal instead of taking his patriotic place among our troops in Vietnam that they sentence him to death and assign his own mortified father to perform the execution. My fourth nominee was such rich movie material that I optioned it myself, wrote a screenplay on speculation, and then submitted book and screenplay to Paramount, which immediately bought them and set about finding a director for what the then studio head felt would be an outstanding picture. He was suddenly replaced, however, and the new chief executive abruptly canceled the production on the grounds that Vietnam might become a "forgotten issue" during the year it would take to make and release the movie. As it turned out, Dick Nixon and Henry Kissinger were keeping the issue very much alive fourteen months later when they ordered their Christmas bombing of North Vietnam.

Years after that, when the war was long over, another producer saw the same comedy values I did in the script and was eager to make it. The rights, however, had reverted to the author of the book, who had expressed great delight with my script and then died suddenly at the age of forty, leaving his estate, including the book rights, to his parents. They, we discovered, were loyal to the side of the family on whom the heavies in the book were based, and they had no intention of selling the rights to anyone.

To those of us who came of age in the 1930s, no event was more critical and partisan than the Spanish Civil War of 1936–39. My own feelings on the subject were, of course, bound up with the death of my brother Jim on the final night before the International Brigade was withdrawn. Liberals all over the world had tried to help the Spanish government prevail, and many felt that its defeat in 1939 made a world war inevitable. But it wasn't until the early 1970s that it became feasible to treat that conflict in realistic terms in an American movie. At that time I proposed a script called *The Volunteer*, based on Jim's story. The same Hannah Weinstein who produced *The Adventures of Robin Hood* during the blacklist was now producing movies at Columbia

Pictures, where the studio head welcomed the project and contracted with Hannah and me for a screenplay and a production to follow. This time, it seemed that no obstacle was likely to stand in the way of what would have been my favorite movie. Then the same commonplace but always-unanticipated blow that had doomed *Farragan's Retreat* at Paramount struck at Columbia: a sudden switch in studio command. The new chieftain told Hannah right off that he hated the idea and would have no part of it. His opinion notwithstanding, it is probably the best script I ever wrote, but its only market seems to be as the fifth entry in my dream festival.

The sixth and final nominee for my festival of unmade movies is called *Death Row Brothers*. It is a true story that Eleanor Jackson Piel, the outstanding lawyer who secured the freedom of two men who had spent eight years awaiting execution, originally told me. In order to make the film as real and gripping as possible, I accumulated a file of newspaper clippings about the case and spent time with the men themselves as well as with all the principal witnesses. There was no reason to concoct a single detail to make the story starker or more dramatic. Law enforcement officers having decided the brothers were guilty, proceeded to doctor the evidence to secure their conviction. Ms. Piel became involved solely out of her opposition to the death penalty, never suspecting she would find her clients entirely innocent of the crime and be able to prove that fact beyond any doubt. With no fictional embellishments whatsoever, the screenplay is a strong indictment of capital punishment.

In the spring of 1998, I was invited to receive the First Annual Writers' Tribute at the Nantucket Film Festival, the only festival I know of that honors writers rather than directors as the major creative force in filmmaking. I was introduced by Frank Pierson, author of many screenplays including *Dog Day Afternoon*, and *Cool Hand Luke*, and director of the *The Looking Glass War* and the Barbra

Streisand remake of *A Star is Born*. He traced the beginnings of the idea that movies were directed rather than written back to the publicity sixty years ago about "the Capra touch." And he reported the reaction of Robert Riskin, the screenwriter of most of Frank Capra's greatest hits, including *It Happened One Night, Mr. Deeds Goes to Town, Meet John Doe,* and *You Can't Take it with You.* Putting together a stack of a hundred and twenty sheets of blank paper, Riskin dumped them on Capra's desk with the words, "There, Frank. Put the Capra touch on that!"

nine

"Grow old with me,
The best is yet to be"

THOSE were Robert Browning's words; certainly they aren't mine. In recent years, my usual response to "How are you?" has been: "Old." It's the most succinct description of how I feel, physically. We go through most of our lives, the lucky ones do, without being too concerned about the minor diseases and injuries that limit our capacities for brief periods. Time, plus a competent doctor and the right medicine, heals most wounds and temporary ailments. But then comes age and a series of afflictions that are qualitatively different in that there are no cures, no roads back to full health. What you look for instead in a treatment is a way to alleviate the symptoms and slow the process of degeneration. The best you can hope for is essentially a stay of execution.

Two such mounting disabilities that began rather early for me were deafness and arthritis. Deafness, of course, can strike at any time or even be present at birth, but is generally associated with age. My own trouble became noticeable before I was seventy. I soon acquired a hearing aid for my right ear, then another for my left ear. Now the right ear is beyond help and the left requires bigger and more elaborate amplification devices with separate transmitter and receiver. And though I have a wireless infrared system for TV-watching and moviegoing, my powers of comprehension are increasingly limited to unaccented English delivered with little or no background noise—a pair of requirements that is scarcely ever met in either medium.

The various problems of old age have piled up with remarkable rapidity. I have arthritic spurs that, despite more than one operation, have left me walking with two canes, and my atrial fibrillation has produced a "silent" heart attack. To contend with these and other symptoms, my daily medical intake includes Zocor and niacin for the cholesterol and Coumadin, an anti-coagulant formerly used as a rat poison, for my circulation. (The rats bled to death but human doses are measured at a much lower level). The benefits of some of these drugs are hard to appraise, but it is a reasonable assumption that without the cholesterol reducers and a low-fat diet, my heart would have stopped working long ago like my father's and brother John's.

So I am resigned to being a cripple for the rest of my life. A deaf cripple, that is. A deaf cripple with a heart condition. Yet there is a sense in which I don't really feel old at all. Part of that must come from my lifelong sense of being the youngest in whatever group I was involved with. In grade school, at Andover and at Princeton, I was always one of the very youngest in my class. I was one of the youngest to be published in a national magazine, probably the youngest city news reporter in New York, the youngest Hollywood publicist and, when Budd Schulberg and I wrote some scenes for *A Star is Born*, one of the youngest writers ever to see his work on the screen. I was twenty-two when my first child was born, and I believe I was the youngest to receive an Oscar for screenwriting in addition to being the youngest of the Hollywood Ten. Anyway, my image of myself is pretty much the same as it was thirty or forty years ago. Even bent over and leaning on my canes, I am taken aback when I tell people my age and they don't act surprised—which they almost never do. And although if anyone asked me about my prospects, it would remind me that a fatal ailment could show up any day, such a thought doesn't enter my head spontaneously. In fact, I often catch myself engaging in unrealistic long-term planning: Should I take advantage of the bargain rates by renewing my subscription for three years not just one?

Another reason I don't think of myself as an old person is that I don't have the sense of being superfluous or in somebody's way. I still do the same kind of work I've always done and I don't feel any less adept at it. I do have a short-term memory problem but long-term memory, which you need for reminiscences, is largely intact though it sometimes takes longer to tap into.

When I was young, I believed in the ability of people to organize themselves in their own interests but also in what seemed to me to be the larger interest of humanity. I thought we had at least the possibility of putting our fears and our superstitions behind us in the interests of creating a better world. When people ask me if I think we could ever end up with a new version of a Red scare—a nationwide purge of dissidents and a blacklist—my answer is usually no, not at least in exactly the same way. But perhaps nothing has surprised me more than the return of the irrational to our political and social life in the form of fundamentalist religious fervor. I tend to think that the strongest threats to the First Amendment now come from the efforts to censor the content of movies, television, art and the Internet that spring from the Christian Coalition and other right-wing religious groups.

Theologians maintain that it is possible to prove the existence of God. This can be done, they say, by two methods. One, known as the First Cause Argument, is based on the premise that every existing thing must have a cause, and every cause, a prior cause. So either you look back on an endless chain of causes or you hypothecate a first cause that does not require a causal explanation. In which case you have presented an argument where the conclusion disproves the premise. The second method, the Argument from Design, was very persuasive indeed before Darwin and the theory of evolution. Thomas Paine, the great prophet of the American Revolution, and other eighteenth-century rationalists called their religious faith Deism. For Paine, the existence of God was a fact proven by the unimaginable beauty and wonder of creation; the story of Jesus, on the other hand, was not supported by credible evidence of any kind beyond the probability that there was such a preacher and that he was executed under Roman law for sedition. There was no eyewitness evidence or even hearsay on the virgin birth or the resurrection, or on Jesus's intention to found a new religion. The various and contradictory accounts of his ministry were written by members of a later generation who never cited the sources of their information. Most important of all to Paine, the whole theology of redemption served no purpose except to justify and enrich "a religion of pomp and revenue, in pretended imitation of a person whose life was humility and poverty."

Paine and other Deists, however, maintained that the evidence of design in the universe was too strong to doubt that it had been created and set in motion by a supreme intelligence called God who then let nature take its course without further divine interference.

The concept of evolution changed all that. For most scientists, the origin of species by the combination of chance and necessity called natural selection was far more plausible than the idea that God created thousands of different insect species with a separate purpose in mind for each and placed (to borrow a figure from Richard Dawkins's *The Blind Watchmaker*) a hundred billion planets in his universe so that on one he could locate a species in his own image and blessed with an immortal soul.

Today, there is a gross anomaly in what is known, perhaps prematurely, as the civilized world. In the words of Sir Frances Crick, who shared the Nobel Prize for determining the structure of DNA:

> The Western culture in which most living scientists were raised was originally based on a well-constructed set of religious and philosophical beliefs. Among these we may include the idea that the earth was the center of the universe and that the time since the creation was relatively short; the belief in an irreducible distinction between soul and matter; and the likelihood, if not certainty, of a life after death. These were combined with an excessive reliance on the alleged doctrines of certain historical figures, such as Moses, Jesus Christ and Muhammed.
>
> Now the remarkable thing about Western civilization, looked at in the broad sense, is that while the residue of many of these beliefs are still held by many people, most modern scientists do not subscribe to them . . . A modern scientist, if he is perceptive enough, often has the strange feeling he must be living in another culture . . . A considerable fraction of the public shows a keen interest in the discoveries of modern science, so that he is frequently requested to give lectures, write articles, appear on TV and so on. Yet even among those who are interested in

science—and many people are indifferent or somewhat hostile—it seems to make very little difference to their general
view of life. Either they cling to outmoded religious beliefs,
putting science into a totally distinct compartment of their
minds, or they absorb the science superficially and happily to
combine it with very doubtful ideas, such as extrasensory perception, fortune-telling and communication with the dead.

The logical case for God is rooted in the idea of a universe with a
beginning. "But if the universe were really completely self-con-
tained, having no boundary or edge," writes Stephen Hawking in *A
Short History of Time*, "it would have neither beginning nor end; it
would simply be. What place, then for a creator?" In the Errol Morris
film version of the book, Hawking adds: "And who created *him*?"

In the contest with superstition, science has made great strides.
Yet some of the most eye-opening discoveries of my lifetime have not
been fully acknowledged by a large proportion of humanity—not just
by the semiliterate and overworked masses of the Third World but by
the privileged intellectual elite of the First. Much of the explanation
for this puzzling failure is to be found, I believe, in the persistence
of a cultural phenomenon that anthropologists say distinguished the
Neanderthal from the beast: religion. Its enduring power, in turn, can
be largely attributed to the urge—as strong in modern as in ancient
times, evidently—to believe that we are somehow exempt from the
cycle of birth, growth, decline, and death that governs every other
form of life.

When I said there were no benefits to old age, I was talking about
physical well-being. There are non-material rewards, and the most
valuable of them is what might be called progenitorial satisfaction.
You don't do anything much—just have some children and help
them grow up, and then the process continues without you. They pro-

duce your grandchildren, who in turn produce your great-grandchildren, of whom we now have four. In 1995, Frances and I were given a joint eightieth birthday party by our five children, and a whole lawnful of other relatives and descendants showed up, coming from as far as England (my daughter Ann) and Los Angeles (my son Joe). My dear friend Paul Jarrico flew in from California, too, with his wife Lia, and the presence of all these cherished people filled us with a deep sense of satisfaction. Not accomplishment, I remind myself, just satisfaction.

Frances, who is my age, was a much healthier specimen than I until 1998, when she was in a serious automobile collision that left her with a variety of injuries from which her recovery is, and will probably remain, incomplete. My doctors, too, have stayed busy diagnosing new maladies and prescribing palliatives that promise increasingly little benefit. As I come to the end of this memoir, Frances and I are both being monitored by a team of care-givers, a state of affairs we don't much like. What disturbs us about the years (or months) ahead is not so much death itself, however, as the events and circumstances leading up to it.

I have a right, of course, not to believe in a soul or an afterlife. Why should I care if others feel differently? What does it matter to me if my neighbor belongs to one of the organized religions or expresses faith in an all-seeing and loving God?

It wouldn't matter much if my neighbor were, in fact, complacent about my rejection of his faith. But, alas, religion imposes a duty on many of its stalwart followers to bring me around to their point of view, willingly or otherwise. Christians cite the words attributed to Jesus Himself: "He that believeth and is baptized shall be saved; but he that believeth not shall be damned."

St. Paul, among other interpreters of Jesus's teachings, has presented those choices as the only ones open to us. If you listen to

Protestant revivalists in America, you will hear variations on the same message: "God requires nothing else from you but faith in Christ and His work to save you immediately for eternity," says an advertisement for the Church of God. "This, the only way to salvation, can be verified by reference to the Holy Scriptures, which are the unchangeable and infallible Word of God. Believe in the Lord Jesus Christ and you will be saved."

Nothing else is required: no character references, no record of good deeds, no indication that you reached your decision after weighing the evidence pro and con. Whatever sins, crimes, and unvirtuous conduct you may have engaged in, you are saved from eternal torture—the fate awaiting devout believers in other religions, people in parts of the world where Christian teaching is unavailable, and all those who, regardless of the noble or altruistic works they may have performed, haven't made a formal commitment to Christ. If you believe that, you accept a God who created humans and urged them to multiply, only to condemn the overwhelming majority of them, after a mere three score and ten years on earth, to everlasting, unspeakable torment. A few years ago, Gore Vidal described in *The Nation* how the monotheists ("sky-godders" he called them) have promoted and sanctified racism, denigrated women and homosexuals, vilified birth control and abortion, stigmatized or criminalized the pleasures of gambling, sex, and alcohol, and distorted the intention of our founding fathers to establish a nation without religious shackles. As he pointed out, only Judaism, the smallest of the three monotheisms, doesn't try to spread its message to the rest of the world. Once securely established, Islam and Christianity set out ruthlessly with armed might to kill or convert every infidel in their paths.

While I am naturally aware of the vast number of kindnesses and charitable acts performed by clergymen, members of religious orders, and ordinary people carrying out their Christian, Jewish, or

Islamic duties, I submit that many of the same men and women, if emancipated from their worship of a supreme being, might behave the same way out of simple human brotherhood. Or sisterhood. In any case, all that good conduct is far outweighed, in my opinion, by the appalling effect that organized religion has had on the last two millennia of Western history—and what it promises for the future. There is no way to add up the death toll from the wars and massacres conducted by the two imperialist faiths, Christianity and Islam, against "pagan" peoples, against each other, and against separatist heresies within their own ranks. The genocidal extermination of the native peoples of the Americas that began with Columbus and Spain was almost always conducted in the name of gentle Jesus. So were various African and Asian slaughters by England, France, Portugal, the Netherlands, Germany, Italy, and Belgium.

The antagonism of religious orthodoxy toward every major scientific discovery in history is well-known. Today in America, in a time of AIDS and spreading venereal disease, Roman Catholics and fundamentalists alike stand stalwart against sex education as well as the free distribution of condoms and clean hypodermic needles. In the last decade of the twentieth century, the number of professed believers has only risen. Most of them have joined the various fundamentalist groups that subscribe to biblical inerrancy and are trying to impose on the country their rigid standards of what is acceptable in art, literature, theater, movies, and television.

But there is a reason more compelling than any of the above for exposing the fallacies of religious belief. To the urgent and overriding need to achieve zero population growth and stop destroying our environment, organized religion, Christianity in particular, presents an even more fatal obstacle than indifference. Christ's emphasis on not thinking about tomorrow has become, with the accumulation of threats to human survival, a doctrine too dangerous to tolerate.

Expressed in its extreme form as apocalypticism, the reason we don't have to worry about the future is that we will soon face Armageddon and the end of the world as we know it. Such prophecies produce apathy among fundamentalists toward every imaginable warning about the environment. But even when expressed in less dogmatic terms, any real faith and trust in a higher power that loves and protects humankind cannot embrace the possibility that that power would ever permit his favorite creatures to destroy their world and themselves. Why should we worry about a hole in the ozone layer when the hand of God could so easily close it before mass melanoma sets in? If we can't figure out on our own a way to dispose of nuclear waste, we can pray to a benevolent deity to provide us with the answer. Global warming may be a problem beyond our capacity, but there are, by definition, no limits on the capacities of God. In the final analysis, even if He chose not to save the world from man-made destruction, only our mortal existence would be at stake. The more important goal of eternal life in heaven would still lie ahead.

I realize that religious individuals and organizations have joined various efforts to preserve the environment, but I don't think believers in a God who can solve everything could apply themselves with the same grim recognition of possible extinction as could completely rational people. And by rational, I mean people with faith in that patchwork product, that supreme result of accidents and necessities on this particular planet, the human brain.

That was where Tom Paine was placing his faith when, two centuries ago, after the French Revolution, he wrote *The Age of Reason*. He was overly optimistic, as some of us still were in 1945, about how soon and how definitely the power of reason would triumph over mythology and superstition. I observed the two hundredth anniversary of his masterwork by recording some of the irrational convictions still prevalent in this country. Here is an abbreviated list. Each claim has a basic improbability about it. None could meet the ordinary standards of proof required in a court of law or an objective scholarly investigation. Yet each is the earnest belief of millions of Americans:

The human species was divinely created a few millennia ago in the Garden of Eden.

The movements of constellations and planets shape human character and influence events on earth.

All illness is an illusion to be overcome by the mind, not by doctors or medicine.

It is possible to foretell future events by means of palm-reading, tarot cards, tea leaves, or special powers bestowed on certain individuals.

Vehicles from other solar systems have visited our planet and sometimes taken earth residents aboard as passengers.

Certain restless dead people, refusing to accept extinction, return to their earthly premises and harass the current occupants.

Certain "psychics" can communicate with one another at great distances by some form of extrasensory perception.

The scientific term "theory" applied to evolution means that the concept is still an unproven issue among biologists.

A second coming of Christ is imminent.

No one will go to heaven who has not been baptized.

The first, microscopic, fertilized human cell already contains an immortal soul that retains a single, intact identity through all the billions of cell divisions yet to come.

A select minority of the world population, mainly in Europe and the Americas, will proceed after death to eternal bliss in heaven.

A vast minority of the world population will suffer the ghastly tortures of hell for the rest of eternity because they never declared their faith in Christ (or perhaps never heard of him).

The Pope is infallible on matters of faith and morals.

An Israelite tribe immigrated to North America in 609 B.C. and built a great civilization of which no trace remained except a set of gold plates discovered in 1822 by Joseph Smith of Manchester, New York with the help of an angel named Moroni.

God selected the Jews as his "chosen people" and aided them in annihilating other nations of people who were equally the products of his creation.

Genuine religious fervor can produce "the gift of tongues," enabling believers to speak and understand languages previously unfamiliar to them.

Black people are genetically inferior to white people except in areas such as basketball, sprinting, long jumping, or running with a football under one arm.

Dreams can and do foretell future events.

There never was a Holocaust.

Homosexuality is a deliberate perversion practiced by immoral men and women in defiance of God's express command.

We, or at least many of us, have had past lives on this planet, details of which some of us are able to recall.

ten Sole Survivor

AS I walked to the platform where Eva Marie Saint had just announced my name, I was aware of a level of applause significantly greater than that usually accorded a screenplay Oscar. The same had been true the previous year when Waldo Salt won his award for *Midnight Cowboy*. We were the first two blacklisted writers to be recognized by the Academy under our real names, and the response from the Hollywood elite, the audience at these events, indicated that what a previous generation had seen as a disgrace, even a crime, was now viewed as something like a badge of honor.

In the nearly thirty years since, that reversal has grown steadily more pronounced. The blacklist has been the topic of plays, documentaries, and symposiums beyond counting, and as the only sur-

viving non-defector among the Ten, I have become an all but obligatory participant in these affairs. I have sometimes grown weary of
the praise, the questions, and the intensity of the focus on what was,
after all, just one part of my life. Living in the past is already enough
of a human temptation without dinner and free air travel being
thrown in, and I would happily trade the plaques and ribbons, if I
could find them, for a deal to produce *The Man Who Loved Children*
or *The Volunteer.*

In a century marked by extreme episodes of political persecution
and suffering, ours was a comparatively mild experience. My nine
months in prison is hardly to be compared to, say, the punishment
endured by Andrei Sakharov or Nelson Mandela. In our own country, the Civil Rights movement addressed injustice and professional
discrimination on a scale that far overshadowed anything we
encountered. Even so, I recognize the importance of providing new
generations with a picture of the extent of repression to which even
a nation conceived in liberty could resort out of mindless panic.

Among the writers, I was one of a comparative few, two dozen at
most, who returned when it was all over to something like the same
level of income and prestige we had enjoyed before the blacklist.
Among directors, the record was worse, though a handful—notably
Jules Dassin and Joseph Losey—went abroad and scored greater
success in Europe than they had at home. It was the actors, on the
whole, who suffered the most. They couldn't operate anonymously or
pseudonymously, and the harm to their careers was generally fatal.

After years of steady work as one of the most familiar character
actresses of the 1930s and '40s, Gail Sondergaard disappeared from
the movies, by reason of her marriage to the director Herbert
Biberman, who was one of the Ten. Howard Da Silva was another
outstanding actor whose movie career was pretty much destroyed.
(He had first been named by Robert Taylor, for expressing political

opinions not to Taylor's personal taste. ("He always seems to have something to say at the wrong time," Taylor volunteered.)

H.U.A.C., at least in the later years of its witch-hunting work, did a reasonably accurate job of identifying those who had actually belonged to the Party. In the television industry, however, the networks and their sponsors did not rely on the Committee for their moral appraisals of personnel. They took their cues, instead, from a band of self-appointed civic watchdog groups that helpfully printed up lists of the untrustworthy. If your name appeared in a periodical called *Counterattack*, published by Aware, Inc., you were blacklisted—unless you went to the same group and attained clearance, which required payment of a fee and an abject recantation of your improper beliefs. Enforcement of the blacklist by employers was dictated by a man who owned three supermarkets in Syracuse, N.Y., and threatened to boycott the sponsors' products if they failed to comply.

Some actors made a go of it by working in the theater, the only branch of the entertainment industry that refused to go along with the whole sordid business. But even after the blacklist ended, few found work in movies or television again. A whole decade of nonappearances on large or small screens was enough to make audiences forget all but the most familiar faces (like those of my friends Zero Mostel and Jack Gilford), and the faces themselves had undergone changes during what could have been critical years for developing a popular following.

Apart from the cost in income and reputation, there was the immeasurable loss of creative opportunity. Before the committee came calling, a few of us had attained the standing and financial security in Hollywood that made it reasonable to think about becoming producers, as a number of our writing contemporaries did in those years. Even when the blacklist took hold, some of us thought it might be possible to make movies outside the usual channels. Mike Wilson, Paul Jarrico, and Herbert Biberman were among a group of my blacklisted peers who set up a production company in the early '50s; then, in a remarkable campaign of guerrilla ingenuity and doggedness, they made a movie called *Salt of the Earth*, against the coordinated opposition of studios, unions, labs, and the federal government, which went as far as to have the leading lady deported midway through shooting. That they completed the film at all was a feat, but the obstacles they had to overcome suggest just how much the scales had been tilted against us. By the time we re-established ourselves (those of us who did), we were in our fifties and hardly in a position to raise money or take heavy financial risks; so we gratefully accepted the jobs that Hollywood, in its new beneficence, offered us.

Paul Jarrico, a friend of sixty years' standing, was not satisfied when the heads of the movie business put an end to a blacklist they claimed had never existed. He thought something should be done about all the screen credits assigned to pseudonyms and "fronts" rather than to the people who had done the work. Paul became the organizer of and moving spirit behind a Writers Guild committee that went through the intensive labor of reading scripts and interviewing those who had written them or who had allowed their names to be used for motives ranging from self-sacrifice to greed. He and his guild colleagues saw to it that record books and, whenever possible, actual credits on still-existing prints were corrected. In many cases, the evidence from testimony and the scripts themselves was too confusing to make firm judgment possible, but the committee managed to establish proper credit attribution on fifty-five films released over that fifteen year period during which the blacklist was in operation.

When the fiftieth anniversary of those Hollywood hearings before H.U.A.C. approached, the committee members decided it would be appropriate for the movie business as a whole to mark the event. Virtually all the major industry organizations and guilds took part in the ceremonies, which were held at the Academy of Motion Picture Arts and Sciences theater in Los Angeles, and many took the occasion to regret that, as Richard Masur of the Screen Actors Guild put it, "the poison of fear so paralyzed our organization." Herbert Biberman was posthumously reinstated as a member of the Directors Guild, and Paul and I received plaques engraved with the text of the First Amendment from Daniel Petrie, Jr., president of the Writers Guild of America, West. It was "in sadness and shame," Petrie said, that he looked back at the guild's own part in enforcing the blacklist.

I was introduced to the gathering with the information that I had prepared a statement to read at the hearing in 1947 but had been forbidden to do so by Chairman Thomas. "And now," said my introducer, "for the first time anywhere, he will read that statement." And I did:

> I wish to speak briefly on two matters which seem to me very pertinent to these proceedings. The first is my own record as it has been impugned by the testimony of some of your witnesses.
>
> My father was a writer in the best tradition of American literature. That tradition is very closely allied to the democratic ideal in American life. Not only I but three of my brothers have also been writers. Two of those brothers were killed in the same great struggle to preserve that democratic ideal, one as a member of the Abraham Lincoln Brigade in Spain in 1938, the other as a war correspondent in Germany in 1944. I make no claim to the genius of my father or the courage of my brothers but I do maintain that everything I have done or written has been in keeping with the spirit that governed their work, their lives, and their deaths.

My principal occupation is that of a screenwriter. I have contributed to more than a dozen motion pictures, among them *Woman of the Year*, for which I received an Academy award, *The Cross of Lorraine*, about the resistance movement in occupied France during the war, the screen version of the play, *Tomorrow the World* about the effects of Nazi education, *Cloak and Dagger*, about the heroic work of our Office of Strategic Services, and an animated cartoon called *The Brotherhood of Man*, based on the pamphlet "The Races of Mankind" and exposing the myth that any inherent differences exist among people of different skin color and geographical origin. My record includes no anti-Semitism, anti-Negro feeling or opposition to American democratic principles as I understand them.

Secondly, about un-American activities in Hollywood. The atmosphere there is considerably different than that of the small segment of Washington to which I have been exposed in the last ten days. Compared to what I have seen and heard in this room, Hollywood is a citadel of freedom. Here anti-American sentiments are freely expressed and their spokesman heartily congratulated. Here there is such fear of the effects of free speech that men are forbidden to read statements and are cut off in mid-sentence lest they expose too much of what is going on here to the public. What I am most concerned about is the ultimate result that might come from a successful fulfillment of your purpose. On Tuesday, the Chairman said that there was subversive material in motion pictures and proposed that it be prevented in the future by an industry blacklist. The motion picture producers have not indicated they are gullible enough to fall for such a ruse, but if they ever did, the fact that I might be prevented from working at my profession would be of little account. The really important effect would be that the producers themselves would lose control over their pictures, and that the same shackling of education, labor, radio, and newspapers would follow. We are already subject in Hollywood to a censorship that makes most pictures empty and childish. Under the kind of censorship which this inquisition threatens, a leading man wouldn't even be able to blurt out the words 'I love you' unless he had first secured a notarized affidavit proving that his leading lady was a pure white, Protestant gentile of old Confederate stock.

The blacklist did plenty of damage, but it was also a broadening experience for many of us. In Mexico, New York, London and Paris, we met people we wouldn't have met and saw things we wouldn't have seen if the privileges and comforts of our Hollywood lives had not been taken from us. Books were written and movies and TV programs made that would never have existed otherwise. Enduring and overcoming the blacklist became a political cause in itself, cementing friendships and creating a new camaraderie. In circumstances that tempered our competitive instincts, people were generous with work as well as money. According to an understanding that developed among some of us, a blacklistee who got offered an assignment he couldn't do himself was expected to pass it on to another blacklistee. Trumbo and Wilson applied this concept to their movie writing on the West Coast, and Ian and I applied it to our TV writing on the East.

The death of Edward Dmytryk in 1999 made me the sole survivor of the Hollywood Ten, and, for a decade before that, I was the only one called on to represent our side of that story. The first of my Hollywood friends to die was Hugo Butler, in 1968. Then, in 1976, came Dalton Trumbo, who was ten years older than me; next Zero Mostel, who was exactly my age; followed by Michael Wilson and the composer Sol Kaplan. Ian Hunter died at the age of seventy-five in 1991.

It was around then that I began to notice a curious phenomenon. After getting used to the death of an old friend or colleague every few months, I found them occurring less and less frequently. A time eventually arrived when I could safely stop turning to the obituary page first thing at breakfast, because there were so few left to die.

One old friend, Paul Jarrico, seemed very unlikely to show up in that part of the paper. At eighty, Paul was in reassuringly fine fettle when I saw him at a lunch meeting of surviving blacklistees in Hollywood three years ago. Emerging from a whirlwind of work on the credit-restoration project, he was in a buoyant state of mind. When the session was over, he got into his car by himself to drive up the coast to his home in Ojai. Tired out from all the activity, he fell asleep at the wheel, ran into a tree and was killed instantly.

That was my last glimpse of him in person. His smile still beams out at me from an eight-by-ten on my office wall, however, directly under the equally expressive faces of Ian and Trumbo. My close friends in Hollywood were in fact a strikingly adaptable and talented group, and they all kept in touch. Somewhere in my files are specimens of the comic verses that used to arrive from Paul every Christmas. (1991, for example, brought us his "Battle Hymn of the Republicans," which included the lines: "we built the greatest war machine the world has ever seen/ we humbled Caribbean isles, taught Libya not to preen/ we could have won in Lebanon if only they'd fought clean.") Paul himself kept everything, as I long ago learned. When M.G.M. bought *Woman of the Year* after Paul had recommended me for the project, I gave him a mock I.O.U for "one career." Seeing me off to prison nearly a decade later, Paul returned the I.O.U. with a fresh notation in his hand. He had written: "Paid in full."